Sunset Manor

Adventures in aging
in a small Midwestern town

Laurel Carey

This book is mostly fiction. The characters in these stories do not represent any living person, they are a combination of the many individuals the author has known throughout her lifetime. The people named in the memoir sections are the only real people in the book, all other named persons are a product of the author's vivid imagination. Some events and locations are factual and some are fiction.

DEDICATION

A big thank you to all my friends in the Forest Lake Writer's Workshop for their weekly inspiration, humor and feedback through the years, to Holly Harden, a great teacher and a wonderful friend and Kelly Paradis who has helped put this book together every step of the way.

This book is dedicated to my late husband Bernie, my three sons, their wives and all the grandchildren they have given me. And to my late friend Mike K and all the friends I have met along my path. Without them there would be no story.

Chapters

Not Where I Dreamed I'd End Up

This is NOT where I dreamed I'd end up. No sir. Not in a two-and-a-half room second floor flat in a subsidized senior complex and definitely not in central Minnesota. No, I fantasized my retirement in some luxurious suite in a fancy, gated community with an ocean view or at least an indoor swimming pool. I imagined myself in southern Florida or a Texas dude ranch or maybe even Hawaii, some place warm and friendly, with no snow and companions that could engage in interesting conversations. But here I am, at age 83, stuck where the residents thrive on TV soap operas, Walmart shopping trips, and in-house gossip. I'm doomed to die of boredom!

I read once that boredom is just a state of mind, so, if I'm going to survive, I guess my real challenge here is how to turn my state of mind around into a state of character study. I've decided to just sit by in the community room and the outside patio as an onlooker observing my comrades, the other inmates housed here. I'll try to discover who they are in their sunset years and what they had hoped to become in their younger years. I'll try to find out what they actually did to achieve their dreams and what they would have done differently if they'd had the chance. Maybe I'll even try to worm my way into their deepest secrets.

Every person over 50 has tucked somewhere in their past, an interesting life adventure just waiting to be told. Given the chance in a trusting environment, most everyone is willing to share these experiences with others. I will strive to put together a collection of some of their stories, their adventures, their opinions and I'll also throw in some of my own. I hope you enjoy this assemblage of stories and viewpoints. Perhaps you may even identify with some of the ideas and experiences.

1

My goal is for you to have a few good laughs and be fed a few bites of food for thought and maybe even cause you to shed a tear or two. (But try not to dampen the pages of the book.)

I live in an apartment in the center building which is called Middle Manor. There are three identical two-story structures side by side. The only difference is the color of the front doors. Middle Manor's door is green, South Manor is a faded blue and North Manor's door is painted rusty orange. I think this was done so that those of us that can't see the house numbers anymore can still identify our own door by the different colors.

The Primary Medical Adviser

I've come up with nicknames for some of the residents here at the complex I've named Sunset Manor. First and foremost on my list of characters here at the home is our Primary Medical Adviser. She has had first hand experience with every illness and human affliction known to the modern world. Just name your problem and she's had it, and her case was even worse then yours. And you MUST listen, because SHE knows. She is then obliged to inform you of the list of medications she has been forced to take and the procedures she's had to undergo to correct her extraordinary ailments, and then she will rattle off the results of each one of these procedures told in their gory details.

Sadly though, none of these cures have worked, because she's developed a whole new set of illnesses and symptoms, and she's back to square one.

The Watch Dogs

Next on my list are the Watch Dogs. They are the occupants that sit at their window and keep a running inventory of the comings and goings of all the residents. They note the time you leave the building and the time of your return. They check out how many bags you are carrying and also from what store these purchases were made. But I've found a way to befuddle them. I once bought a robe for my daughter-in-law from Vanity Fair Lingerie and I kept the bag. I did the same with a shopping bag from Fredrick's of Hollywood and a cloth carrying bag from a well know liquor store nearby. So, while I'm still in my garage I transfer my grocery purchases to these three bags and then I flaunt my way across the parking lot to the front door. They always seem to be in the hallway and we meet at the elevator, accidentally, of course.

"Oh, I see you've been shopping?"

"Yes." I answer in a coy manner. "I just had to pick up a few things I'll need for a party I'm invited to on Saturday night."

I leave the rest to their imagination. Tongues must have wagged that weekend, because I did get some sideways glances from the folks in the laundry room on Monday morning.

Oh My, I've Lost My Keys

Next I'll Introduce you to Oh My, I've Lost My Keys. The poor dear loses one of her keys at least once a week. She's lost her house key, mailbox key, car key, safety deposit key, strongbox key and a variety of other keys. Why she carries so many kinds of keys I can't imagine. If she carried them all at once she would look like a jail warden. But they must all be on separate key rings because she is always looking for only one key at a time. We have all suggested she put her important keys, like her front door key, her apartment key and her mailbox key on the same key chain. "That way you will have all your necessary keys with you at all times," we have said to her.

3

"Oh my, no," was her answer. "That way if I lose it I will have lost them all!" We must to patient with her; she is quite elderly and still lives alone.

"Well then," we have suggested, "set a basket just inside your door and as soon as you enter your apartment, drop your keys into the basket and that way you'll always have your keys close by."

"I tried that," she explained, "but I forgot where I set the basket. You see, I didn't want strangers to see where I keep my keys."

I can understand how she might have lost the basket in her apartment; it's so cluttered it would be hard to find anything. The same thing has happened with all her remotes.

She lives in the building next door, but one day she met me at Middle Manor's front door and asked me to come to her place to help her select the remote that controls her air conditioner. She had in her hand a plastic grocery bag containing seven remotes.

"What are these all for?" I asked.

"I don't know," she said, "I've tried them all and none of them will start the air conditioner."

"Well Jenny, none of these are air conditioner remotes, they're all TV remotes," I told her. "How many television sets do you have?"

"Only one," she answered, looking weepy.

"Which one of these remotes is for that TV?" I asked out of curiosity.

"I'm not sure. I have to try them all before I find the right one," she laughed, in spite of her teary eyes.

"Jenny, why don't you throw away the useless ones and just keep the one good one? Then you won't get so mixed up," I suggested hopefully.

"Oh, I don't know, I always think maybe someday I'll have use for one of the others."

We never did find her A/C remote, but we did discover my remote works on her A/C as well, so whenever she wanted to change the temperature or mode on her machine, she would call me and expect me to run to her apartment to accommodate her needs. The building owner finally bought her a new remote, so I'm off the hook at least for the time being, but I have started checking my caller ID to make sure it is not her on the other end of the line. I know that sounds selfish, but I just can't be running across the yard every time she forgets were she has hidden something or misplaced something. She's going to have to learn some responsibility. Or do you think it might be too late?

Monday she lost her car keys (yes, she still drives) but she found them on Wednesday when she was looking for her mailbox key, which she found the next day while looking for her air purifier remote. And so it goes.

The Puzzle Man

Puzzle Man is obsessed with assembling jigsaw puzzles. He works diligently on the puzzle he has picked out, until the picture is completely assembled. Then he will stand over it and admire his accomplishment for a moment or two, but almost immediately he will break it down and begin another.

He enters the community room each day with a large thermos pot filled with hot, strong coffee. He walks into the room confidently and goes directly to "his" puzzle table like a man on a mission. He opens the puzzle box and tips the cut pieces of a beautiful picture out on to the table top and lovingly turns all 1,000 parts face up. He studies them carefully and then begins to sort them into separate piles. Edge pieces into one pile, sky pieces into another. There will be piles of bright colors and shades of green and blues. House parts and people parts are put into their own piles.

The sorting done, he scans the picture on the box cover and then the assembling begins. He will take a sip of his coffee, adjust his thick glasses and, with the tip of his tongue anchored securely between his teeth, he sets to work. He chooses each piece carefully, caresses it lightly with his bony fingertips and places it into its proper place.

He will work diligently, sometimes four or five hours at a sitting, leaving his rolling chair only for nature's call. His chair on wheels maneuvers easily around the puzzle table and at spaced intervals, he interrupts his concentration to pour a steaming mug of his fragrant brew and then sip it contentedly. His coffee mug is always close at hand. He will be patient and industrious until all 1,000 pieces are in their proper order. It may take two days or ten days, but no matter, he will continue to persevere. When he has finished the complete picture, he will stand back admiring his handiwork. He will smile at his achievement and then carefully disassemble it, placing all the tiny parts back into the box for safe keeping.

I think it is not so much the victory of his accomplishment that he savors, but more the playing of the game.

The Compound

There are 18 apartments in each one of the three identical structures and each building has its own black-topped parking lot. There are single garages available for the small percentage of the occupants that still drive cars. The complex of multiple brick dwellings is located on about a quarter acre of landscaped property on the outskirts of a fair sized city. The backs of the buildings sit about 25 feet from the property line which borders a thick, brushy pine and poplar woods, with a few scattered old oaks.

As far as apartment houses go, this complex is above average in care and management. It is privately owned and the paid cleaning person keeps all the common areas hospital clean. She vacuums the halls every day and I'm surprised there is any knap left on the carpeting. The south building looks out over a hayfield and the north views the small city's skyline. Across the parking lot and main road, there is a cattail swamp, a bird watchers paradise.

Shopping is easily accessible for the non-driving residents by using the senior bus that picks up passengers at Middle Manor parking lot every Tuesday morning at 10:30 a.m. and returns them at 2:30 in the afternoon. This bus will bring the weekly group of shoppers to a small shopping mall and the grocery and other stores in the area. Our complex has privacy, yet it is convenient to the local clinics and hospital.

Signs, Signs, Everywhere Signs

There are signs tacked everywhere. Notices giving detailed instructions on every aspect of our life here. As you move down the hallway, you will notice there are name plates on every door. Sometimes there is a welcome sign stuck beside the occupant's name. Some doors even have personalized knick-knacks hanging on the outside of their doors from metal hooks placed over the top of the door itself. This hook is a must, if you want something on the outside of your door, because there is a large warning sign on the laundry room bulletin board which reads: "DO NOT PUT NAILS INTO THE DOORS!"

There are personal notices stuck to the inside of the front door with scotch tape. I wish people wouldn't be so Scotch with their tape (ha ha) because the notes are usually dangling there by one ear, and they read like this: "Birthday Party Tomorrow." Well, what day will tomorrow be? When was this note put up? Whose party is it? What time does it start? Usually no useful information accompanies these notices. No wonder nobody ever shows up.

There are "Do Not Enter" signs on too many hall doors. The storage room door and the elevator maintenance room door, the furnace room door, and the utility room door. Do we really need those signs? These doors are always locked up tight anyway.

There is also a professionally printed notice on the outside of the laundry room door stating the hours the laundry is to be used and hand written notes on the inside of this same door reminding occupants to: "Please remove Kleenex and sharp objects from pockets before washing." And one above the dryer stating: "Clean filter after each use!" And still another telling us: "Don't forget to take your clean clothes to your apartment."

Back in the front hall you will see signs that tell you: "Don't forget key in mailbox," "Don't block front door open," "Don't leave unwanted junk mail on bench," "Don't! Don't! Don't!" There are more "Don'ts" here than there are "Do's."

Just inside the front door there is a sign shouting: **NO SMOKING IN THIS BUILDING.** Then another sign tacked nearby that reads: "Please put your cigarette butts in the receptacle." (Hey, you're not supposed to be smoking in here!) Yet another sign plastered to this receptacle begs you not to put candy wrappers into the butt container.

Four steps and you're outside. Here there are several tall metal signs concreted into the curbing with more orders: "Resident Parking Only," "Handicapped Parking Only," Loading Zone Parking Only" and "Emergency Vehicles Only." There are only six parking spaces along this curb. Where the hell is a common driver supposed to land? No sign for that.

The community room in Middle Manor is on the second floor. It's a nice, big, brightly lit room, well equipped to accommodate the residents to gather for parties or meetings or to just sit around and talk. But only a few take advantage of this convenience. Sadly, a large percentage of our residents seldom join in any of the activities in the community room, unless there is free food offered. Then they simply come in to fill their plates, eat silently and go back to their caves. But there are a small handful of women that do assemble several nights a week to play cards and enjoy each others company. And the older man that spends much of his time working jigsaw puzzles at the same table every day.

Sunset Gossip Club

We have a large concrete patio on the west side of Middle Manor with a glass top table, outdoor chairs and pleasant surroundings. Some residents have planted pots of blooming pink and red geraniums and there are containers with purple petunias hanging from shepherd hooks along the edge of the cement slab. A plastic hummingbird feeder with colored liquid hangs enticingly from a low branch of the ornamental crab apple tree. There is also a bird feeder for the smaller birds like goldfinches and chickadees. This feeder is a long plastic tube filled with black sunflower seeds enclosed in a wire cage-like contraption, to keep the big birds from eating all the seeds. At this time of year, the thin September sunlight filters through the autumn leaves of the apple tree to make dancing patterns on the grass below.

It is 2:00 p.m. Gossip hour. Three lady residents and I sit contently hashing over the week's happenings at our senior building.

The subject is the same event we've discussed every afternoon this whole week. My attention is only half on the conversation around me. I've heard it all several times before. I am much more interested in the activity of an industrious little chipmunk as he cautiously maneuvers his way down the steel rod of the wire-caged bird feeder hanging from a limb of the tree. The feeder is filled with glossy black sunflower seeds and the little chipmunk is determined to find a way into the wire cage. He climbs around the side of the cage and somehow squeezes between the bars and now sits happily stuffing seeds into his cheek pouches. As I watch him, it brings to mind the children's story of Peter Rabbit and how he ate so much in Farmer Brown's garden, that he wasn't able to squeeze back out through the hole in the fence. If Chippy keeps stuffing seeds in his mouth like he is doing, I wonder if he will find himself in the same fix?

Someone speaks my name sharply and I am jolted back into the circle of the conversation. When I looked back at the feeder, the little fellow is gone.

Moments later, I feel something on my foot, making its way up my pant leg and to my surprise, Chippy scampers onto my lap. One of the women lets out a blood-curdling scream, pointing at my lap. She jumps off her chair so suddenly it topples over with a crash.

"Rat! Rat!" she shouts, waving her arms in the air. All the commotion frightens the poor little guy and he promptly scampers off into the bushes.

We all have a good laugh, except for Fran, who is frightened of all four legged creatures. But the diversion was great. Now we have a new subject for tomorrow's conversation.

The little chipmunk comes around at gossip hour every day now and is fed far more than his share of goodies, compliments of the "Sunset Ladies Gossip Club."

Crabby Applebee

Nobody really likes her here at the apartment house. She's never pleasant to anyone. Residents avoid meeting her in the hallway because she always has something to complain about. She is habitually negative and her face has a permanent scowl etched across her brow. Behind her back we call her "Old Grouch" or "Crabby Applebee." She seldom comes to any activities in the community room and when she does attend, it's only to air one of her new complaints.

My first encounter with her came the third day after I'd moved into my second floor apartment on the first day in February. While I was putting my cooking supplies away, I dropped a bag of sugar and it broke, spilling out on a kitchen scatter rug. I rolled the rug up and took it to the back door to shake out the sugar.

For security reasons there is a sign on the back door requesting the tenants not to leave this door open. I had no intention of leaving the door open, I was only going to give the rug a quick shake and duck right back in. I had propped the door open only a crack with the hall broom so it wouldn't completely close while I shook out the rug. I was standing about two feet out the door when a loud, angry voice shouted, "Don't prop this door open!" The broom was promptly kicked out onto the snow covered patio, and the door slammed shut.

I wasn't yet accustomed to always carrying my door key, so I was locked out. A cold winter wind was blowing across the patio. I had no coat or boots on and was standing in the snow in my stocking feet. I finally made my way around the building through a foot of snow, to the front door where the door bells are located. I wasn't acquainted with any of the residents, so I just pressed the first button on the doorbell panel. It was for unit 101 and the kind occupant let me in. Thank goodness it wasn't old Grouch's bell. As time passed I learned it was best to just avoid this woman.

There are several small garden plots available behind our building and both she and I and five other residents plant flowers and vegetables back there. The plot she has claimed is at the corner of the garden area, nearest the back door and her apartment unit. Her plot has always had saggy green plastic fence surrounding it. It looks trashy, but she feels it will keep out all the thieves and trespassers. This year I noticed her area is completely choked with crab grass and weeds. Her four spindly tomato plants are almost hidden in a forest of weeds. Her hanging geranium is wilted from lack of water, while her glass rain gauge is over flowing. Something must be wrong, so I start asking around.

"Oh yes, haven't you heard? Her two aunts, her only living relatives, have both recently died," another resident tells me. I also learn she had never married and had spent her whole life caring for her sickly parents. After they'd died, she had moved here. I realize she must be lonely and maybe even a little bitter, and she probably never learned how to communicate with other people. I also found out that besides losing her aunts this month, she had just undergone knee surgery and was unable to keep up her garden on her own.

Mustering up my courage, I knocked on her apartment door. My heart was pounding with dread. Will she spit in my eye and tell me to mind my own damn business?

It took her a while to get to her door, enough time for me to change my mind and disappear down the hall, as my lack of courage was urging me to do. She opened her door just a crack. "Well?" she snarled in a suspicious voice.

My fear made me speechless for a moment and then I just blurted out, "I, I was out weeding my own garden and, and, and I finished mine, and, and I was just wondering if you'd mind if I did your garden too?"

She stood in her doorway, staring at me for several moments, leaning heavily on her one crutch. Those few minutes seemed to stretch into an hour. Then two large glistening tears slipped from her faded blue eyes and slid down her wrinkled cheeks.

"You'd do that for me?" she spoke almost in a whisper, but then her demeanor grew gruff again. "I don't have a lot of money you know," she grumbled, "I can't pay you much."

"I don't want any pay. I only need something to do," I said, and quickly added, "so it's okay if I pull your weeds?"

"Yes. Oh yes, that would be really good of you. Really nice," she whispered gratefully and her voice cracked.

I worked in her garden the remainder of the day and she stood in her picture window and smiled and waved at me every time I looked up. She invited me to her kitchen and fed me a tuna sandwich and ice tea. She chatted endlessly about the beautiful gardens she used to grow when she was a young girl and lived in the country.

It took me two days to finish the work needed in her plot. She had opened her window and pulled a chair close so she could visit with me through the screen. She warned me not to work too hard or too fast and she insisted I come and sit outside her window and rest in the shade every so often. She kept me hydrated with a steady supply of ice tea. Her whole personality seemed to have changed and I actually began to enjoy her company. One day a week or so later I found a homemade "thank you" card taped to my door with a

14

packet of flower seeds: Forget-me-nots.

We still visit in the hall when we meet, but she seldom comes to any of the activities in the community room and she still grumbles a bit. I also discovered that she likes to put on her gruff facade in the presence of the other residents. I learned from that experience that you never really get to know another person when you choose to hold yourself at a safe distance from those that seem difficult. After that summer, I felt privileged to know there is really a kind and caring heart beneath that well camouflaged exterior.

Winter Trash

We had an extreme amount of snow last winter and I was thankful to have a garage to park my car inside. The residents who own a car but do not have a garage must run outside and brush the snow off their cars and move them from our parking lot to somewhere else whenever the handyman decides he is ready to plow our parking area. So much snow fell last winter, the snowplow had nowhere to push it except up onto our front concrete patio.

We all welcomed the spring because it had taken its time getting here. But now it is the second week in April and the days are finally warming enough to start to reduce the six foot high mound of dirty snow which has been stored on the patio since the autumn blizzard. The pile had increased in height all winter, until I couldn't see over it.

I was unable to reach my bird feeders the whole winter long and the little chickadees and the blue jays would perch in the leafless crab apple tree and scold me for my negligence. The snow had piled over halfway up the bare trunk of the apple tree and there was no way an old lady like me could make my way over that mountain of icy snow chunks. As a result, the feeders were empty most of the winter.

Now after several weeks of mild days, the accumulated snow mountain has reduced itself down to a pile of messy debris. Two lonely lawn chairs have resurfaced, their plastic covers torn and ragged, their metal backs pointing hopefully towards the sun. The chairs have been moved to the dry sunny spot at the southern-most corner of the concrete patio slab. They accommodate the more hardy residents already hoping to soak up some vitamin D from the thin spring sunshine.

I snoop around a bit in the scattered litter spread out across the patio blocks, and you'll never guess all the bounty the north wind has blown onto our summer retreat.

All winter the snow from our parking lot has been pushed up onto the patio slab and the huge pile had served as a windbreak from the strong north wind. The discarded debris from the street would blow across our cleared parking area and lodge itself into the great snow bank.

With the toe of my sneaker I nudge at the accumulated piles of rubbish. There is a multitude of McDonald's and Wendy's hamburger bags, gum wrappers, pop cans and empty cigarette packages. There are heaps of advertising pamphlets and junk mail. I kept wishing I'd find a five or ten dollar bill, but no such luck.

I did find one treasure that really struck my funny bone, though. It was a plastic Ziploc bag with a neatly folded pair of black lace pantyhose. Tucked inside the clear plastic bag along with the hose was a handwritten note taped face up, which read: "Found these in my back seat."

Hmm...now where do you suppose the wind could have picked up such an item in a senior parking lot? I might, with a stretch of my imagination, consider it possible if it had been white elastic medical hose or beige knee-highs or even long tan cotton stockings, but a pair of black lacy pantyhose? No way.

I asked around the complex, but needless to say no one in the buildings has claimed them. As a joke, I tacked the evidence up on the "lost and found" bulletin board in the laundry room. I thought it might give some of the residents an incentive.

By the way, they're still tacked up there, now with a few risqué remarks attached.

Ants

In the summer, I spend a great deal of my time on the back patio of my building. It's always peaceful back there and it is a good place to quietly reflect on the past and mentally restructure my future. No one else uses this quiet space except Mary Lou and me. I no longer use the garden plot because it is so overrun with creeping charlie and alive with our famous Minnesota mosquitoes. I have instead planted seven containers of flowers. Some of them hang in plastic pots from the shepherds hooks, while others sit on the built in benches or directly on the cement floor. There are tall shade trees surrounding this area so it gets very little sunshine to nourish the flowers, but they seem to be surviving.

I've planted twelve cucumber plants in an enormous clay pot, sitting on a wooden platform with wheels. Several times a day I go out and move the whole darn thing to the sunniest spot on the patio, hoping it will catch a few extra rays. It's not doing too well.

Mary Lou and I share maintenance duty out there. I take care of the plants and bird feeders and she keeps the concrete floor swept and the table and chairs wiped clean of tree and bird debris. We never really discussed this arrangement, it just fell into place. We are rarely both outside at the same time. She is a late riser and an indoor person and I like to be outside in the morning to drink my breakfast coffee in the fresh air.

One morning, as I relaxed in a lawn chair, I noticed our patio seemed to be home to a large variety of different kinds of ants. They were working their way out of every crack in the concrete floor. I like to watch the ants scurrying around, helter-skelter on the cement slab. They seem to all be in such a hurry. Maybe the floor is too hot on their little feet. Sometimes they are heading north across a patio block, only to suddenly make a 180 degree turn and head south again. They never seem to know where they're headed and they never seem to get to their destination. There are so many different sizes of ants on our patio racing about. They range in size from large carpenter ants a quarter inch long, to tiny grease ants about the size of a grain of salt, and every size in between.

What are they thinking, I wonder? Do they really know where they are going? Why do they work so hard and never seem to make any progress? What are they always looking for? They must have the answers, but they sure don't act like they do. Scientists say ants are extremely intelligent and equally industrious, but I'll add another fact that's not in their book-- they are damn near impossible to get rid of.

They remind me of the bargain hunters at discount stores in shopping centers. They're all rushing around looking to find the best buys, dashing from one store to another. When I direct my attention to just the tiny ants, I almost have to laugh out loud because they act like the teenagers on the prowl at the malls.

They move around in tight little groups and then cautiously venture near the bigger species, to observe them, I suppose, but then they seem to become alarmed and scatter, only to regroup and repeat their maneuver over and over.

I've purposely dropped a crumb of bread on the cement floor, just to see what they would do with it. Sometimes one will spy my offering and try to drag it away. They must have some form of communication, because soon there will be an army of their kind, all working together pulling the tidbit one way and then another. I've never noticed them getting the crumb to any special place, but when I take note of them again, like magic, they are all gone and so is the treat.

I know this seems like a foolish pastime, but it is a cheap and interesting diversion from a long, boring summer afternoon.

Minnesota: The Early Years

While lounging in the shade on this quiet back patio, I often replay the memories of my youth, wondering where I'd be if I had played my cards differently.

I was born in this small town in central Minnesota at the start of the Great Depression in the 1930s. My father was lucky to have a job with a local road construction company as a heavy equipment mechanic. This type of work meant our family was forced to move around from town to town, to wherever my dad's job was located. Back then, they called what we lived in a "construction caravan." This was a group of families living in separate company bunkhouses. A bunkhouse was a one room wooden structure set on wheels. It served as the sleeping quarters for each family. They were much like the modern day trailer houses, except without any of the conveniences. It had no cooking facilities. All the cooking was done by the wives of the employees in a common bunkhouse appropriately called the cooking shack. This rustic cooking trailer had two kerosene cook stoves and an ice box built into the interior, which held three or four solid chunks of real ice. The drop down tailgate was used as a serving bar. The cook shack also carried all the cooking supplies and utensils. All the families ate in shifts at long, portable tables outside the cookhouse. If the weather was bad, we took our food to our sleeping quarters and ate our meal sitting on our bunks.

I never started a school year in the same town two autumns in a row. I'd start school in whatever town my dad was working and then, about the end of December of that year, I would transfer back to the Raymond school district to finish out the term. I was a poor student and never reached a grade above a C. (Oh, maybe a B in recess). The Raymond teachers told my parents I was mentally slow, but my folks felt I did poorly in school because I was blind and cross-eyed in my left eye. I'd been injured in a freakish accident when I was only three years old. My left eyeball had been cut badly by a broken medicine bottle while I played with another youngster in her back yard.

It was obvious I did have a learning disability because I had to struggle so to read, yet I loved books and reading was my escape. I was often teased by some of the other children because my left eye was so crossed, but I don't ever remember being unhappy in my childhood years. I had a great imagination and I could pretend my way through any difficulties.

When World War II was declared, my family moved to the Twin Cities area and both of my parents went to work in an ammunition plant making hand grenades for the military. They worked there until the end of the war in 1945.

While attending school in the Minneapolis school system, the real reason for my inability to read was discovered. I am dyslexic. This discovery had an upside for me; it taught me to focus more carefully and read slowly and concentrate. At age fifteen, I had surgery to correct my crossed eye and that was a life changing experience for me. I lost my self-consciousness and I became more outgoing and self assured. My high school years were wonderful. I will always be blind in my left eye, but I can live with that. I graduated from Miller Vocation High School in 1948, completing all required high school courses and my Cosmetology course. I was licensed and worked as a manicurist in the Dayton's department store's Looking Glass Salon for approximately six years.

While still in high school, I met and then married Bernie Carey. We were both only eighteen years old, but we were happily married for thirty five years. I lost him to pancreatic cancer in the summer of 1983. He was only 53 years old.

Flagpole

As I mentioned earlier, I'd spent my younger years in a small town in central Minnesota. The town had only one playground for the kids to use during summer vacation and it was located behind the school on school property on the northeast edge of town. I never quite understood this ordinance, but the playground equipment on the school property was off limits to the kids living on the south side of town across the railroad tracks.

I know it sounds crazy, but the city fathers felt it was too dangerous for the unsupervised lower class children to cross over the railroad tracks to play on the school yard equipment during summer vacation. The south side children crossed these tracks twice daily during the school year, so go figure?

Well, we south side kids had lots of grassy fields and friendly yards to play tag and kick-the-can and stick ball, so we really weren't hurting for places to play, we just didn't have ready made playground equipment.

One afternoon Keith, my best friend and also my cousin, had to visit the dentist's office and I got bored being alone. I hiked over to the city water tower park to just hang out and watch the highway traffic. It wasn't really a park, only a triangle of grassy land set between the main highway and two side streets. I liked to lie in the thick grass and watch the heavy grain trucks drive past on their way to the tall grain elevators on the east side of town. Sometimes if they noticed me sitting on the curb and they would toot their loud air horns and wave to me.

As I lay in the grass below the city flagpole, I was thinking as I stared up at the 48 stars and stripes. My eyes began to follow the cable down the pole, from where the flag was clipped to it at the very top, down to where it was looped

22

over a hook which was welded to the pole. The pole itself was a fat iron pipe cemented into a concrete base buried deep into the ground.

If I put my foot in the loop of the cable and gave myself a little push, I'll bet I could swing out a bit, I thought to myself. I got up from my comfortable spot and wandered over to the pole. I unhooked the cable and put my scuffed tennis shoe into the loop and shoved off. It worked! I swung out about three feet and around the pole once. I'd only given myself a light push the first time, so I pushed a little harder the second time, and sure enough, I swung out over ten feet.

Soon I was launching myself twelve to fifteen feet out and going around the pole five or six times. As the cable wrapped around the pole it brought me closer and closer to the concrete base, but just before it was about to stop, the cable would begin to unwind itself and would swing me out again in the opposite direction. As the flagpole began to sway, it seemed to fling me out even farther. I was almost sailing out over the bridal wreath bushes that hide the little park from the view of people passing by on the sidewalk.

I was absolutely enthralled, giddy with delight. I was lightheaded and in a fantasy world. I'd never felt so free, so weightless. I had the sensation of being an eagle soaring high above the clouds, gliding on wind currents. The summer breeze caressed my cheeks. I felt as light as air. When the cable finally settled and I was able to step off onto the slab and down to the ground again, I was energized, breathless and dizzy. I lay down again on the grass and closed my eyes, still holding onto the glorious sensation of sailing through the air.

"Flying the Flagpole" was never shared with the uppity-up kids from the north side. We south side kids kept this sport strictly to ourselves. But we discovered it could only be a summer activity, because when the boulevard bushes lost their leaves, our secret playground became open for all to see. We knew the city fathers would never approve of our activities in Water Tower park, so we closed down until next season.

Urgent Care

I only wanted to talk to my primary doctor for a minute about a small concern. Nothing earthshaking, just a question. But of course I had no luck.

One of the most irritating situations in my life these days is the inaccessibility of our medical professionals. We're told by the medical industry that they are readily available when one needs advice or some supposed knowledge on problems regarding one's health. But where can we go to get these answers? If you call one of the nurse help lines, regardless if you think it's a big problem or an insignificant one, your answer will eventually always be the same. After spending twenty minutes explaining your concerns, the person on the other end of the phone will wisely advise: "I think it would be best if you would have someone run you to your closest Urgent Care unit. Thank you for calling."

If you take this advice and you drive yourself to the hospital and check yourself into the Urgent Care unit, you will wait in the lobby at least an hour or more before you will be ushered into an examining room, where you will wait another half hour. You will soon begin to wonder what "urgent" really means in these modern hospitals.

If you don't show up at the Urgent Care facility, but opt to call your primary doctor's office instead, your phone call will more than likely be answered by an automated answering machine. After the fourth ring it will kick in and an upbeat voice will say: "If this is an emergency, please hang up and call 911. Thank you. Have a nice day."

Oh yeah, like you'd be calling them if you were having a nice day.

The phone will then continue to ring another five or six times. Oh, thank God, a human finally answers, but before you have a chance to speak, the receptionist beats you to the punch. "Please hold!" she orders. After waiting another five or six minutes, while being entertained by elevator music which is interrupted at intervals for the medical center to advertise the procedures they offer, suddenly the phone line goes dead and you're hearing the dial tone again.

You hang up and regroup. Who was I calling? What was it about? Oh yeah, my blood tests, the ones taken three weeks ago. They said they would call me as soon as they knew the results. Oh God, it must be bad news, it's taking so long to get the results.

Now you start worrying. You go to the kitchen to refill your coffee cup and return to your desk. This same routine will repeat its self another time or two and by now, it's not your blood test you're concerned about, it's your blood pressure.

You start over. The phone is finally answered. "Medical clinic, please hold one minute," you're told.

"Go to hell!" you scream into the phone and slam it down. You won't die of any known disease; you'll just explode from frustration.

Back in the "good old days" the doctor's office was right down the street, above the corner drugstore, across the hall from the dentist's office. His office had three or four small examining/treatment rooms. The reception room had four or five straight backed chairs and a couple of high backed overstuffed chairs, so you could lean back and be comfortable. There were hooks behind the door to hang your coat. In the center of the room was the nurse/receptionist's desk. Usually the nurse was also the doctor's wife. Your health files were stored in steel cabinets along the back wall.

You didn't have to wait for weeks to see the doctor because he didn't take weekends off for golf tournaments. Usually your appointment could be made for the next day, but if it was "urgent care" you needed, you were encouraged to come right in. You never had to spend much more than twenty minutes in the waiting room because as a patient came out of an examining room, Mrs. Doctor would rush in to clean and sterilize that room, preparing it for the next patient.

This small town doctor treated almost everything, with complete confidence. He would have a very high success rate as well. He could stitch up wounds, set broken bones, deliver babies, treat cold sores, pneumonia, pin worms and influenza. I do realize some of today's illnesses and the medical treatments and techniques are much more complex than they were back in the 1930s and '40s. And I do admit we now have more serious illnesses, ones never even dreamed of back then. But many of these afflictions have been brought on by our own lack of self-care, carelessness and indifference. The attitude by some practitioners nowadays is: "I'll write you a new prescription. Take these pills for a day or two. That should take care of it, if it doesn't, we'll try another unproven drug." I think that's why they're called "practicing" physicians.

The present day primary doctors treat almost no illnesses right in their clinics. I'm almost convinced their function is to make referrals to their colleagues, the specialists in every imaginable field.

If you have an ingrown toe nail, it's off to the podiatrist. A headache, you're sent to a neurologist. If you get a rash, you go to a dermatologist. A bellyache you're off to internal medicine. And if you're too fat, they'll just cut out a piece of gut, no problem.

If you're experiencing heartburn, you will be sent to see a heart specialist who will recommend you walk the treadmill, have an EKG, an ultrasound, chest x-ray, carotid artery scan and many other tests. But don't worry, they will give you plenty of prescriptions, like Coumadin and Plavix to thin your blood and surely you'll get one of the many pills offered to lower your cholesterol, even if your cholesterol isn't high. Never mind about recommending healthy foods and a simpler lifestyle, just take a handful of capsules--that should do the trick. That is, if you can survive all the procedures.

I apologize for coming down so hard on the modern day medical community, but I've had some really bad experiences. I'm probably a little jaded. I do realize people expect doctors to do miracles and I know that isn't possible.

And I also know many doctors nowadays can do wonders, but I also wonder what many doctors nowadays really do?

Guide Your Days

Guide your days so there can be
a goodly bit of charity,

Not just the sharing of your wealth,
but the generous giving of yourself.

Someway, each day, fill someone's need
by thought, or word, or kindly deed.

Then keep the word of the deed inside,
away from temptation's boastful pride.

Recalling Kisses

I'm trying to recall my very first memorable kiss. It could have been the one from Tommy Nelson on Grandma's front porch the summer I stayed with her at the farm.

Surely not, I was already thirteen years old. I must have been kissed before that. Oh, now I remember, it was the summer before that, when Byron kissed me behind the corn crib at the Sadie Hawkins Day dance. But even before that, Bobby What's-His-Name tried to kiss me in his dad's row boat, but just as he puckered up, a wave from a passing motor boat hit the stern and he planted his sloppy lips right above my left eye. That was one encounter I'd rather forget. Once I got a kiss from Daryl Dunn back in the fourth grade. He gave me a shy smack on the corner of my mouth on Valentine's Day. The same day he gave me a box of candy wrapped in a newspaper and tied with fish line, but then he ran away before I could kiss him back. I could have run after him and caught him, because I was a much faster runner then he was, but I didn't bother. The candy, as I remember, was really good.

Now that my memory has kicked into gear, I can recall a whole multitude of insignificant kisses over the next five or six years. But when I was about seventeen and a junior in high school, I was asked to attend the high school prom by my school hero. He was the star basketball player and he drove his own 1946 maroon Mercury coupe. The dance turned out to be a flop, but I had a marvelous time. What has become indelible in my memory was his good-night kiss at my front door. Wow, what a kisser. But the biggest surprise was when my dad threw open the front door and whispered: "You dumb kids, you're leaning on the door bell. You want to wake your mother?"

Two yeas later, I was that superb kisser's wife. As time marched on we exchanged many kinds of kisses over the next thirty five years. A peck on my cheek when he left for work each morning. A good-bye kiss when he was going on a business trip and romantic kisses when he returned. There were sweet and gentle kisses exchanged between us and our three baby sons, and then later among the growing family of grandchildren. There were kisses of sympathy at times of sorrow and kisses at joyful occasions, like weddings and births and baptisms and private nights out and private nights in.

But I struggle with emotion when I recall the kiss that will stay anchored in my heart forever. Our last kiss.

Losing Bernie

My high school sweetheart and I eloped when we were both eighteen years old (well, he was almost eighteen). We hitchhiked, along with our best friend, to the town of Northwood, the first county seat over the Minnesota state line into Iowa. That was on November 28, 1948 and we traveled there in a full blown Minnesota snowstorm. But we kept warm. We were in love.

We spent our first 25 years in different homes in Minneapolis and during that span of time I gave birth to three beautiful and healthy sons, about four years apart.

In 1974, we moved out of the city and bought 120 acres of property along Rock Creek, a picturesque setting 75 miles north of the Twin Cities and began building our retirement home, a hobby farm. In several years, we had accumulated a menagerie of farm animals: two saddle horses, a mixed breed dog, cats, ducks, chickens, an African goose named Freda, and of course, Bernie's pride and joy, his herd of eight Hereford cows with calves.

Bernie continued to commute to his office in the city. In 1979, he had a serious heart attack, brought on by the stress of the long daily drive and his demanding job as a business agent for the local electrical union. Three years later, he was diagnosed with pancreatic cancer. In those days there were few treatment options, so the next 14 months were a nightmare of drugs and chemotherapy, surgeries and pain, both physical and emotional. He lost weight rapidly and by the spring of 1983 had gone from a robust 200 pounds to a mere 102 pounds. He never lost his beautiful black hair, but he did become diabetic.

I became skilled at giving him his daily pain, insulin and preventative medicine shots. But he was losing his battle with the dreaded disease. The chemotherapy was not slowing the growth of the tumor and it seemed to be making him sicker, rather than helping him fight the battle for his life. So one day he just told the doctor: "Enough." All curative treatments were ended, but he still continued the pain medicines and the insulin shots.

We were now faced with the painful task of preparing for death. There was no hospice care available in our area so I cared for him as best as I could at our country home. "No more hospitals," he had told me.

We set up a hospital bed in front of the living room picture window. From there he could watch the birds at the feeders, the eagle soaring in the summer sky and his prize Herefords grazing in the front pasture. I also hung the hummingbird feeders in his line of sight. Hummingbirds were his favorite winged creatures. With the windows opened wide, he could hear the gurgling of Rock Creek as it made its way down to the St. Croix River, only a mile away.

One day, I was dozing in my chair with a book in my lap, when I heard him softly call my name.

"Yes dear, I'm right here." I answered.

"Come sit by me." he said, just above a whisper.

I walked to his bedside and he reached out with his thin, weak hand and took mine. He turned it over and pressed his cracked lips to my palm. I was overcome with emotion. I climbed onto the side of the bed and lay down beside him. He put his arms around me and drew me close to his skeletal body. I pressed my cheek against his haggard face and he turned his head to place his lips on mine. He kissed me lightly at first, but the pressure grew stronger and we clung desperately to each other, while unchecked tears flowed down our faces, blending and wetting his pillow.

He passed away three days later, but the memory of that last kiss will live permanently in a special chamber in the center of my heart.

Setting Fence

I knew him well the spring we set the fence line, when the frost first left the ground. I knew his thoughts as we drove the steel shaft into the moist earth with the aid of the post pounder, lifting and dropping the heavy tool over and over again, until the steel post was driven a foot or more into the cold earth. Every muscle in my fifty year old body was shouting "stop!" And my back refused to straighten, but we had to finish the job.

I knew him even better after the two weeks it took us to replace over a mile of posts and to re-string the barbed wire fence along our north property line. Last winter's snowmobile riders had cut the fence so they could use our pasture as a shortcut into town.

We'd labored all day in the balmy spring sun, but now we were losing daylight. "Let's wrap it up for today," he said, and so we stacked our tools. I climbed up into the passenger's seat and settled behind him, winding my tired arms around his waist. He revved the motor and we took off in a cloud of dust.

I knew this man well, as I lay my dirty cheek against his sweaty back and I closed my eyes. This scenario brought back a memory of another time and place.

I knew him back in 1965 when we were riding a second hand Triumph motorcycle in an open field in the shadow below Bear Butte. It was our first and only Sturgis Rally experience. His memory must have kicked in too, because in the twilight of that spring evening our weariness lifted, and reminiscence took over.

I knew his mind as he began doing figure-eights in the middle of our pasture, on a dilapidated three wheeler. He stopped the machine and we dismounted. He folded me in his tired muscled arms and drew me close. We were young lovers again, laying in the dewy, wet grass, drinking the morning's cold, bitter coffee from a plastic thermos.

I knew him as we lay together on the hard ground, looking up into the heavens, pointing out the stars we recognized, as we recalled the good times in our thirty plus years of marriage.

I know him still, though he is gone now. He lost his courageous battle with cancer, but before he died I wrote a poem for him, comparing our life together with the brave little pink wild rose.

Our Rose

Bernie, our life is like the wild rose,
Not the long stemmed beauties,
But like the tangled little rambling rose
That grows along the roadside.
The one that must push up through the cracks in the
tar.

They stand against all obstacles
Yet they bend with the storms.
Our rose doesn't wither at the first sign of drought,
It stands tough.

It is the kind of bloom that shares its meager space
with other species.
It has thrived in all conditions,
And still gratefully displays its delicate blossom to
the Creator.

Our Rose is the kind whose fragile beauty,
Outweighs its thorny stems.

Have A Nice Day

"Well, have a good one," was the advice the mail delivery man offered me as he left our building. He was the third person to use that cliché on me already today.

Don't people ever say things like, "Have a nice day," or "Hope your day goes well." Or "See you soon?" No, now days everybody says, "Have a good one."

"Thanks." I answer, but I'm wondering, have a good what?

A good lunch? A good afternoon? A good bowel movement? A good strong drink? A good romp in bed? Have a good one, what? Of all the useless comments tossed around at us every day, I think this one is at the top of my list.

Now, if the statement was actually completed, it would make some sense. "Are you taking a day off this week? Well have a good one." Or "I hear you're having dinner out tonight. Have a good one." Or maybe even something suggestive like, "Oh, so you're off on another honeymoon? Well, have a good one."

I just don't see the sense of simply stating "have a good one"' without even giving a clue about what good one they want you to have.

"Like" is another word that drives me crazy. Like, kids nowadays, like, can't start a sentence, like, without using the word "like". Like old people like me, like, just can't catch on. Like we really care.

Quentin

It was an unusually hot summer day, and I had come outside earlier to make sure the patio was vacant. I was looking for a place for some quiet time alone. I'd noticed the flag on the pole in our front yard was waving slightly so I figured there must be at least a little breeze outside. I plopped down on the glider and kicked my shoes off. The white metal glider was placed in the only shady spot left on the patio. I leaned back and closed my eyes, rocking the glider back and forth ever so slowly. A cool whiff of a breeze danced lightly over my face and I knew this was going to be a peaceful afternoon.

I had just begun to unwind, when I was startled out of my tranquil state by a high-pitched cackle.

"Yoo-hoo," shouted Lucille, a boring woman from the south building. I label her boring because her only subject of conversation is her baby-faced grandson, Quentin.

"Quentin has the highest IQ in his school! Quentin was on the Dean's List two years in a row! Quentin was voted, 'Most likely to succeed' and 'Best Looking' in his class year book!"

Quentin is in college now but the bragging still goes on and on. "He picked a college in St. Paul so he could be near me, his dear old Nana," and she punctuates each statement about "sweet Quentin" with a silly giggle. It's always "Quentin this or Quentin that" until I have to get up and leave before I barf.

"Yoo-hoo," she shouted again. I'd kept my eyes tightly closed, hoping she'd think I was asleep. She made her way across the expanse of grass which separates our two buildings. I had no escape. I braced myself for a hour of Quentin praise.

"I saw you sitting out here all alone and I knew you'd just love to hear what my sweet grandson is doing for me today. He's going to be staying with me for a whole week. He just loves to come here to help his Nana, you know. He's always so thoughtful and kind. He offered to take my old rattle-trap to the car wash to clean it up for his Nana," she said breathlessly followed by another giggling fit.

The old so-called rattle-trap is really a 2004 Cadillac with everything electric and only 32,000 miles on it. All those miles probably are from going back and forth to pick up dear, sweet Quentin from his private schools in Minneapolis.

Lucille and I sat and chatted for about an hour. Correction, Lucille chatted, I just sat. Finally I asked, "Where did Quentin take the car to wash it? If he just took it over to the car wash on this end of town, shouldn't he be back by now?"

The next scene I will never forget. The words had just left my mouth, when the caddy pulled into the parking lot next door and stopped. No one got out of the car. There sat dear, sweet Quentin in the driver's seat, covered with soap suds and soaking wet, his beautiful, blond curls dangling around his head like a wet string mop. He was crying like a baby.

Lucille ran to the car, "Oh, darling boy, what in heaven's name happened?"

"Oh Nana," he sobbed, "I got the code numbers and pulled around to the car wash entrance and rolled down the window to punch in the code numbers, and then I did what the sign told me to do. When the light turned green, I pulled up onto the conveyer track and put the gear into neutral and turned off the motor. The conveyer track grabbed the car and pulled the car into the washing stall

40

and the water started spraying. But the motor was off and the window wouldn't go up and the washer started washing and the brushes started brushing and the soap started spraying and I couldn't get the window up, so me and the inside of the car got washed too. And I'm soaked. And the lady wouldn't give me my money back. And they all laughed at me." He burst into renewed sobs.

Lucille just stood there staring at him. Then she realized what had happened.

"Oh, for God's sake, Quentin, stop bawling like a baby. You're an idiot, do you know that? Do you realize you've ruined my beautiful, expensive car? All my money is invested in this car."

I had to leave the scene quickly or I would have made a fool of myself by laughing out loud in front of them. Quentin's mama and daddy picked him up in less than a half hour and no one has seen Lucille outside for the past three days. The "rattle-trap" is hidden in the garage, out of sight.

Traveling Pop Can

It was now late August. The sun had slipped across the cloudless sky and was moving slowly west. I slumped down in the lounge chair on the front patio. I was trying to muster enough energy to move myself out of the chair and up to my apartment because it was getting close to supper time. The traffic on the street, which runs past our parking lot, had thinned to only a few cars going home and the trucks heading back to their home terminals. The padded lawn chair and warm sunshine had lulled me into a light doze.

Suddenly the crash of a metal pop can hitting the concrete pavement jarred me wide awake. I sat up, wondering what had happened. And then I saw it, a lone Cola Can rolling helplessly along the curb. Each time another vehicle sped by, the empty can was pulled back and forth across the street.

My childish imagination began to churn. I wondered, what will happen to this can? Where will it end up? A story began to form in my mind:

The Traveling Cola Can

They were all packed tightly into a cardboard container. They were so close together they didn't even have wiggle room.

"Boy they really squeeze us together, don't they?" remarked the aluminum Cola Can.

"Well, we are all stored in 12 packs, you know, and our manufacturers don't want us to jiggle around too much, you know, because shaking us could cause us to explode, you know, because we're all full of carbonation, you know." explained Lemon-Lime, the know-it-all. She was squeezed into the carton right next to Cola Can's pack.

"Where do you suppose they'll take us?" asked Cola Can, to no one in particular.

"Oh we'll probably go to a convenience store or a vending machine someplace. It don't much matter to me, I won't be there long, my brand is always the first to sell because I've got twice as much caffeine as any of the rest of you," bragged a green can of Mountain Rain in its raspy voice.

"Well I wouldn't be so proud of that fact," spoke-up Strawberry Diet soda in her sweet and syrupy drawl. "I only have half as many calories as any of the rest of you, and I contain NO real sugar."

"The real fact of the matter is," declared Root Beer, "we've all been created pretty much equal. Our ingredients are much the same. It's only our artificial flavoring that makes us taste different and just the print on our cartons that make us look different."

All the sodas were quiet after that remark.

Soon the delivery truck stopped and the double doors in the back of the truck were flung opened. The driver unloaded a variety of different kinds of soda onto his two wheel cart and proceeded to restock a vending machine stationed just outside the door of the Dollar Store. Cola's 12 pack was one of the first cases chosen to refill the machine.

"What happens to us now?" Cola Can asked the soda can rolling down the slide track on his left.

"We just wait in line until someone puts a dollar in the machine and chooses one of us. Then we roll down the chute and pop out," she said. The vending machine was filled and the door was closed with a slam and all went quiet and dark.

"What happens if no one chooses me?" Cola Can whimpered, getting a little panicky.

"Well, then you just stay put until your expiration date and then they just toss you out, I guess," a cranky sounding can three rows over said to him.

That didn't turn out to be a problem for Cola, because that very afternoon an old beat-up Ford pickup pulled up in front of the Dollar Store. A dude in cowboy boots hopped out and sauntered up to the vending machine, inserted his dollar bill and punched the cola button and out rolled the soda just ahead of Cola Can. Then the dude stuck another dollar in and pressed the same button and Cola Can was ejected from the machine into the waiting hand of the cowboy.

The first can was opened immediately and Cola could hear the guy guzzling down the cold liquid without even taking a breath.

"Awaaaaaaaaaaa!" Cola heard the dude exclaim and then heard a loud burp. The empty can went sailing out the open truck window. The fellow must have been really thirsty, because he reached over and picked up Cola Can and popped its top.

This time the guy drank more slowly, savoring the cool beverage, but when Cola's can was empty, out the window it went flying.

Cola hit the pavement with a crash and then rolled from one side of the street to the other, ending up with a bang as it hit the concrete curbing. It lay there dazed, but just then another car passed. The drag of air caught the empty can and pulled it along the curb for several more yards. Finally Cola Can stopped rolling amid a pile of discarded hamburger wrappers.

A huge semi truck flew by and the suction from those big wheels scattered the paper wrappers and pulled Cola Can another half block in the opposite direction. Now Cola Can lay among a variety of objects right out in the open and was stuck in the hot sun for the next three days. Cola Can felt extremely warm and was sure its aluminum sides were beginning to melt.

The next day the sky grew thick with dark clouds and thunder rumbled in the distance. Suddenly the sky opened up and the rain poured down. Dirty water started flowing past the clump of discarded waste and Cola Can was quickly picked up by the rushing water and swept along with the rubbish. Closer and closer it flowed toward the open sewer grates, but just as it was about to be sucked down into the opening, the grate became clogged with debris. Cola Can was now pressed tightly against a used Pamper on one side and a spent condom on the other. By the time the storm ended, Cola Can was covered with muck and was half filled with dirty waste water that smelled of dog poop and garbage.

By mid-afternoon the next day the city street crews were out cleaning the clogged sewer drains. Cola Can had almost given up hope of ever being rescued from all this muck, instead worrying about were it would eventually end up.

"Will I be thrown into the village landfill? Or will I wind up on a garbage barge to be dumped into the river? Who cares?" sighed Cola, "it's over for me now anyway." The soda can had given up hope.

But before the city dump truck had reached the pile of waste, an old man on a three wheeled bicycle with a small trailer hooked behind him pulled up beside the debris pile and with plastic gloved hands, plucked up Cola Can from the trash heap. He dumped out the dirty water and then tossed Cola Can into his trailer. The cart was almost filled with rescued aluminum soda cans.

"What's going to happen to us now? Where will this guy take us?" worried Cola Can

"Oh don't fret, little can," called the multitude of salvaged cans in the collection trailer. "We've been rescued by an ecology-minded citizen. He is going to take us to the recycling plant. We've all been given another chance to serve."

"Gee," thought Cola Can, "this is great news. But if I'm given a choice this time, I think I'd rather be a Spring Water plastic bottle next time around.

Truly Good

I have the privilege of being acquainted with a truly, authentically good person. In the years I have known her, I can honestly say I've never heard her badmouth a single person, not even her bossy husband. She never swears, she never grumbles and she never criticizes or scolds anybody. I wish I could be a little more like her. She sees something good and worthy in everybody she meets. Her name is Mary Ann and I sometimes, just in fun, call her Sweet Nurse Mary Ann, because of her caretaking nature. I also refer to her as Mary Ann Manners because she is so ungodly courteous.

Her sweetness puts us all to shame. She seldom makes any kind of demand, but when she does ask for something, the request is always preceded with "please" and ends with "thank you." She is forever apologizing, always saying "I'm sorry" but for what I don't know. She never does anything that would require an apology. When our Wednesday night group of ladies are playing cards she nearly drives me crazy with her thank yous for every card dealt her. If you have the opportunity to play a card on one of her runs, which is the object of the game, she will honor you with a thank you even though a thank you is inappropriate, and certainly not necessary.

If you should happen to sneeze, before you have time to open you eyes, she has a box of Kleenex at your elbow. It you cough or clear your throat, a Dixie cup filled with water instantly appears. She just can't seem to help being constantly helpful. If we are serving food in the community room or having some kind of party, she automatically becomes the waitress.

It's no wonder she is so thin. She's not in perfect health herself, but if she hears of anyone in the building being sick, she is the first one on hand to offer help. She will offer to make you soup or run your errands or bring your mail, absolutely anything at all. She is an earth angel.

You must understand, I love Mary Ann dearly just the way she is, but I wouldn't want all my friends to be quite so perfect. If everyone you come in contact with was always so kind and thoughtful, you'd never have to do anything for yourself, face challenges or make tough decisions. Real life needs tests and trials to build character. We don't need actual physical conflict to grow, but we do need to experience difficulties, weigh opposite opinions, disagree on different points and have personality struggles to learn how to function successfully among other people. If we're always cozy and agreeable with one another, I would have to come to the conclusion that one of us is slow.

The thought of never disagreeing or having a good argument with somebody really scares me. Wouldn't that make life too boring? I feel total and absolute harmony is not really good for one's growth. We need to get our blood boiling once in awhile to build up enough steam to keep us moving forward. If we had only perfect people around us and we all lived smooth and undisturbed lives, life would be too predictable. I thrive on a little conflict now and then.

New Renter

Excitement is running rampant through our apartment building today. A new tenant is moving in. A single man at that!

As the Mayflower moving van backs slowly into the loading zone, five curious and overly excited women line up along the front windows of the community room. They all have the hope of getting a firsthand look at our new male resident.

1. "What's his name? Anyone know?" asks lady number one.

2. "Wonder how old is he," inquires number two.

3. "Do you think he has money?" asks the third.

4. "Hell no, Flora, he wouldn't be moving in here if he had money. Any fool knows that," says lady number four.

5. Number five just sighs.

The back door of the moving van is pushed open higher and the curious onlookers jockey for a better view of the contents inside the truck. As the moving men begin carrying the furniture out of the truck and setting it on the front sidewalk, the watchers upstairs begin jostling in earnest for the best viewing positions at windows.

1. "Boy, he's got a nice couch," says lady number one.

2. "Hey, look at his sound system. He must have at least six speakers," adds lady number two.

3. "So much beautiful furniture. He must have money," suggests number three.

4. "Where is he going to put all that stuff in that little apartment?" wonders number four.

5. Number five just sighs.

Another car pulls up next to the truck and a middle aged woman hops out and hurries around to the passenger side, but first she opens the rear door to lift out an aluminum walker.

"Ohhhhh!" An audible groan passes through the group at the window.

1. "Oh darn, he uses a walker."

2. "Well Hannah, so do you. So what?"

3. "He's maybe just had knee surgery and won't have to use it for long."

4. "It only means he won't be able to tap dance." Giggles erupt from the group.

5. Number five just sighs

The middle aged woman opens the passenger door and slowly two legs emerge from the front seat area. A heavily ringed hand grabs the walker handle and pulls a scrawny angry-looking man to a standing position. As he moves slowly away from the side of the car, he is already shouting orders to the moving men: "Get that furniture into the building and out of the sun, you stupid bunch of hillbillies."

The five women turn and look at each other, first shocked, then questioningly.

1. "I don't think he'll work out."

2. "Maybe you're right."

3. "He is going to be a problem."

4. "You can say that again."

5. "Oh, no ladies, I don't think he'll be a problem. He's just tired. Maybe he's not feeling well."

All four women turn to her and in unison reply, "Oh Mary Ann, get real." But he was a problem, and he still is.

Otto Schmitt

Otto Schmitt moved into the apartment right below mine and then proceeded to set up his surround-sound system that must have been meant for an auditorium. When he turns it on, which is every afternoon and evening up to 10:00 p.m. and beyond, it causes the pictures on my walls to tilt, the bottles in my medicine cabinet to dance and the jars on my dresser to jitterbug.

I don't want to deny him his music, but does he really need the volume set at that level? The vibrations can be felt throughout the whole building. It annoys all the tenants but everyone is afraid to complain to him because he has an explosive temper.

After two weeks of hearing that pounding in my ears and the jiggling of the floor, I decided to ask him to please turn the volume down. I squared my shoulders and marched downstairs. The sound was even louder on the first floor. I tapped on his door. Then I tapped a little harder and finally I ended up pounding with all my might.

No answer. I knew he was in there, but the music was so loud he couldn't hear me knocking. I walked to the doorbell panel in the front entrance and rang his bell. Not once, but three times. He finally poked his head out his hall door and I rushed back down the hall to catch him.

"Otto! Hey Otto, can I talk to you for a minute?" I yelled over the music.

"What?" he answered.

"Can I talk to you, please?" I said as loudly as I could.

"What the hell do you want?" he yelled back.

"I just want to ask you if you'd please turn your music down a bit?"

"What?"

"Please turn your music down!"

"What?"

"Turn the damn volume down!" I hollered.

"Go to hell you old broad and mind your own business!" he shouted at me and slammed the door in my face.

Well, I don't stand still for that kind of abuse so I raised my battle flag. I knew there wasn't much more I could do, because several other tenants had already gone to the landlord about the problem and nothing had been done.

I'll have to declare subtle warfare, I thought. I'll have to think of a way to get my point across to him without conflict.

I bought a packet of sticky notes in bright colors and colored markers. Every day I would write four or five notes: "Volume DOWN Please!" and stick them to his door. I did this for two weeks straight, and then one afternoon I realized the volume was lowered and my floor wasn't vibrating. I wrote one more note, a yellow smiley face and the words "Thank You!" and placed it on his door. The maneuver wasn't a complete victory, but it was a big improvement.

Spiderman

It was raining as I pulled my van into the first available parking space and jumped out. I made a mad dash for the entrance of the discount store. I was in a hurry to pick up a few last minute necessities: milk, cereal, my prescription refill at the pharmacy counter and a birthday card for my granddaughter.

I took the wet shopping cart that was offered me, more to lean on than to tote my few intended purchases. Weaving through the maze of late afternoon shoppers, I headed straight for the dairy aisle. Just as I was about to reach into the dairy case, I was startled by a blood-curdling banshee scream. At the end of this aisle an all too familiar battle campaign being played out.

"I want Fruity Loops! I want Fruity Loops! Fruity Loops! Fruity Loops!" screamed a red-faced little blond cherub, kicking and waving his arms frantically. I stopped at my end of the cereal aisle, not wanting to get too close to the battle field.

"I want Fruity Loops," he continued to shout.

"Stop this right now, Billy, it is not acceptable behavior. I will have to give you a time out if you don't stop," his mother threatened calmly.

Billy went right on screaming, "Fruity Loops, Fruity Loops," at the top of his lungs.

"Oh, alright darling, but just one box, that's all."

The rampage stopped on a dime, and their cart moved on. I proceeded into the aisle and grabbed my half gallon of milk and then in the next aisle a box of cereal, the heart healthy kind, and made my way to the birthday card racks.

And who should I meet again but the Fruity Loop kid and his mama at the Halloween display counter.

"Let's get you this cute pirate outfit," the mother was suggesting over ear splitting screams of "Spiderman! Spiderman! Spiderman!"

I quickly moved on, not wanting to see the results of this encounter. I chose my birthday card, picked up my waiting prescription and wheeled my cart in the direction of the exit lanes. I tossed a few unplanned purchases into my cart basket as I made my way from the back of the store.

When I reached the checkout counter I found myself right behind you know who. He sat contently in the child's seat of their cart with a triumphant smile spread across his little freckled face. He knew how to play the game and he'd played his hand successfully. His mother looked frazzled. In Billy's cart I noted several boxes of Fruity Loops, a Spiderman costume, Builder Bob carpenter's tool set, plastic baseball bat and accessories on a shrink wrapped piece of cardboard, plus a big bag of assorted jelly beans. There were a few items for Mom too--a giant economy sized bottle of extra strength aspirin, anti-aging cream and a box of "Get Rid of Your Gray" hair coloring.

I paid for my purchases and made for the exit doors, but not quite fast enough to avoid hearing one more outburst.

"I want McDonald's! McDonald's! McDonald's!"

As I gratefully passed through the outer doors, I met another young mother on her way in, her warrior already shouting his demands.

I left the parking lot disenchanted. Whatever happened to the word spelled N-O? Don't young parents ever use it anymore? Do they even know what it means?

Bank Joke

Mary Lou had a funny experience last week at her local bank and she shared it with me over coffee this morning.

She had stopped in to make a withdrawal. She walked up to the writing counter in the middle of the lobby and selected the proper slip to be filled out. When she finished this task she planned to bring the slip up to the teller's window to initiate her intended transaction. She chose the appropriate slip and picked up the pen from the counter top to fill in the proper information. Finishing this task, she tossed the pen in her handbag and turned to approach the teller's cage, only to be stopped in her tracks. To her shock and embarrassment, the pen was attached to the counter top by a light chain and now so was she and her purse.

A bank guard walked over to her laughing and helped untangle her. "That happens pretty often," he told her. "We did discuss taking the pens off the chains, but we decided these little episodes brighten up our work day and give us all a good laugh, even if it is at the customer's expense," he said as he gave her a little wink.

"Well, it won't happen to me again, that's for sure," Mary Lou stated with conviction and a little snicker. She said she left the bank a bit red faced and somewhat rattled.

Gunfire After Midnight

There was some excitement here in the middle of the night last night. I was awakened by what I thought were gunshots. In a matter of minutes the building parking lot was swarming with police cars and emergency vehicles. It was about 3:30 in the morning and there was the sound of heavy feet running up and down our hallway. A policeman outside on the front sidewalk was shouting instructions to the occupants of Middle Manor through a bull horn: "Attention residents, stay in your apartment, and lock your door. We have everything under control. Stay calm."

Stay calm? What the hell is going on? Were those sounds gunshots or what?

I tried to see through the peephole in my apartment door, but that view is so distorted all I could see were the wall lights and the door across the hall.

Now I was really getting concerned. I could hear Mary Ann crying hysterically and Helen, from the far end of the hall, shouting in an angry voice at one of the policemen.

"What do you mean it's nothing to be alarmed about? I saw the gunman," she said.

"No, there were no gun shots fired. It was something entirely different that caused the noise in the downstairs hallway. You can all go back to bed now. Everything has been taken care of and all's clear," the policeman said.

By 5:00 a.m. the halls were cleared of all emergency personnel but crowded with speculating residents. They congregated at the ends of every hallway. "Maybe it was a pipe bomb." "Could have been pop cans exploding." "It was probably firecrackers."

"No! It was revolver shots." insisted Helen, "I saw the gunman."

Whatever it was, it scared the life out of poor Mary Ann, who was still white as a sheet, sniffling back tears and blotting her red and runny nose with a Kleenex.

When daylight arrived and most of the renters had calmed down and had gone back to their apartments, the true story finally emerged.

It seems Fred, from a first floor apartment, has no car and he runs his errands on his bicycle. He had ridden to the convenience store down the block to pick up a loaf of bread. When leaving the store he noticed his bike tires looked low on air, so he stopped at the air hose outside the store and put a little air in each tire, just for good measure, and then peddled his way home. It was an unusually cold night so Fred decided not to bring his bike around to the back of the building to the bike stands, but to bring the thing into the hallway until morning. Well, the ice cold bike tires began to expand in the warm hallway. The warmer the tires got, the more they expanded and the result was BANG! BANG!

Well, that sure as heck blew a hole in the gunman theory, didn't it?

House Plants

My mother loved house plants. As a child, I remember our homes were always filled with growing plants. In their later years, my dad actually built my mom a small greenhouse on the south side of their last home.

I like living plants in my life too, but there is not much room to grow things in a two and a half room flat. I do have a very large and old philodendron plant growing in a big orange mixing bowl. It's placed on a plant stand at the side of my double picture window, the only window in the living room. The plant is huge, a full two feet in diameter and it cascades down the side of the stand and spreads out across the carpet under the window.

It has taken over this whole space and is really quite spectacular. It takes very little care, just a good drink of fertilized water once every week or so. Its beauty dominates the whole room. In one corner of the room, on top of an open-sided bookcase sits a huge glass fish bowl holding an enormous Boston fern. Its fronds reach nearly to the ceiling, while the other fern leaves point gracefully down towards the floor. This plant is also easy to care for and is green the year around. It's plastic, but it looks more real than most real ferns and I can clean it by simply setting it in the shower stall and giving it a good rinse.

I also like cut flowers, but they seldom last more than a week, so I have a beautiful square glass vase filled with pink, white and ruby red gladiolus to grace my dinner table year around. They're made of silk. All I have to do keep them looking good is give them a good hard shake and they are ready be on display again. The African violets in my bedroom are of the same species--shake and go. It makes life much easier if I want to take a trip somewhere for a week or so. All I have to do is give Phil an extra big drink of water and she'll do well on her own until I return.

I must admit though, about every two or three weeks I buy a live bouquet of some seasonal blossoms at the grocery store. I know it's kind of extravagant, but I buy them for my favorite person to enjoy. Me!

The Flower Show

Ten pretty flower girls standing in a row,
Each with the flower she had helped to grow.
Amy's Sweet Alyssum blooms in white and purple hues,
It spreads across the pathway and covers up her shoes.
Polly's yellow Pansy has a jolly smiling face,
And Vickie's dainty Violet takes up very little space.
Gerri grows Geraniums with blossoms big and red,
While Barbara has Begonias in her flower bed.
Florence planted Four-O-Clocks in her kitchen window box,
And Margie's golden Marigolds grow in square and even rows.
Sweet Peas are Sophie's favorite flower; they climb along the wall
While Hazel's double Hollyhocks stand up straight and tall.

No one planted Sunflower seeds by the garden gate,
They were scattered by the birds and only grow by fate.
Now here it is, the Judging Day of the Flower Show,
 Ten breathless maidens faces all aglow.
Who will be the winner? Who will claim the prize?
Hope fills every pounding heart and dances in their eyes.
"Who has brought this Sunflower, this giant bobbing head?
This is really splendid!" all the judges said.
"Who will take this ribbon? Who can claim this prize?"
With that a flock of Chickadees darted from the skies.
Where is the Golden Trophy? It's snuggled in a nest,
Because the Giant Sunflower was the very best.

Penny Cookies

Have you ever tasted penny cookies? When my sons were still all little boys, penny cookies were their favorite. My husband worked the night shift at a flour mill in downtown Minneapolis and on his way to work each evening, he would pick up several boxes of donuts at a nearby bakery to be eaten on the night crewmen's breaks. In the morning he would bag up the leftover donuts and bring them home to us.

Now you must realize these boxes of donuts were already about four hours old when he bought them and now had been sitting opened for another eight hours on the job, so even with a stretch of imagination, no one would call these fresh donuts. So I would slice them about ¼ inch thick and set them out of sight until later in the day.

By the time the boys were ready for their afternoon snack of cookies and milk, the penny cookies had dried out just enough to be crisp and flaky. Some were coated with powdered sugar and some with chocolate. Others had cinnamon and sugar. I liked the plain ones the best and they were strictly original.

My boys are now all fathers and grandfathers themselves, but they still love penny cookies and actually buy bags of donuts to slice and let dry out to make their own versions of penny cookies.

My Trip

When my husband passed way on August 16,1983, all three of my sons came to the farm to help me arrange for his funeral and to help fill out all the paperwork that needed to be done.

Bernie was now released from all his pain, but I suddenly realized I was only 53 years old and a widow, alone and seemingly without a purpose. I realized I still had all the farm chores to do and the animals to feed and the yard still had to be cared for, but I tended to all these chores like a zombie, functioning on automatic pilot.

By mid-September all the paperwork had been completed and I just sat on Bernie's bed, crying and staring out the window, wondering, "What do I do now? Who am I? I'm no longer a wife and my children are all grown and gone. I have no job, so what do I do next?"

My former friends had all moved on with their lives. I felt like I was totally lost. Totally alone. After several weeks of useless tears and self-pity, where I'd sit in the dark and drink wine (and I didn't even like wine) it finally occurred to me, I'm still here, I'm alive and I'm really not that old. I've got to pull my self together and move on.

I decided to take a trip to Fargo, North Dakota to visit our friends, the Cameron's. Tom had been our best man at our elopement marriage 35 years ago. He'd attended Bernie's funeral and at that time invited me to come to North Dakota for a visit anytime.

After milling this idea over for a couple of days, I thought, if I drive all that way to Fargo, I might just as well go a bit farther on to Aberdeen to see Bernie's South Dakota relatives. I hadn't seen them in years and they did remind me to visit in the sympathy card I'd received from them several weeks earlier.

Around the middle of September, an old friend, who lived in Dallas, Texas, called me and extended an invitation to come and spend a week or two with her and her family.

I had never traveled long distances alone before, nor had I ever even registered myself into a motel. Well, I thought, I'm alone now so I better get used to doing these things for myself. As long as I'm driving west, I might just as well go all the way to Dallas. It can't be that much farther; it's only about two inches on the map.

My sons were not in favor of my traveling so far alone, so I almost abandoned the idea of taking the trip. But one night, as I lay awake in bed, I had a strange feeling that Bernie was there with me, telling me to be brave and go for it. So in spite of my sons' disapproval, I decided to take the trip. I hired a neighbor and his son to watch my farm, pick up my mail, feed my faithful old dog and the cats and keep an eye on the livestock in the pasture.

I packed three suitcases and a cooler filled with food. I set four large jugs of my own well water on the floor behind the front seat. (I'd heard bad things about water in other parts of the country). I took snacks and a blanket and pillows, in case I couldn't find a motel. I hadn't yet discovered there are more motels than there are people in some states. With my atlas opened on the passenger seat and my planned route outlined in yellow marker, I set out on my life-changing journey at 5:00 a.m. October 1,1983.

The intended route was from Rush City, Minnesota to Fargo, North Dakota and then on to Aberdeen, South Dakota. I wasn't too sure of my itinerary after that. I'll just play it by ear, I thought.

I took many side trips, checking out old forts and historical battlefields and beautiful meadows of wildflowers. By the time I reached Aberdeen I'd left my planned route far behind. I got lost almost daily; sometimes I couldn't even find the original highway I'd been traveling that day.

It was wonderful. I loved it. I didn't care if I got lost, I wasn't on a strict schedule, so I just kept heading down whatever road I was on and eventually I'd come to a town. I'd find it on the map and revise my day's destination.

I did learn a few lessons about picking motels. Small town Ma & Pa places were always good. They were smaller and cheaper and sometimes kind of old-fashioned. Some of them had patched sheets, but the linen was always clean and usually there were good eating places somewhere nearby. If you had to go through a city, it was always wise to drive straight through the town and find a place to rest on the far side. That way you'd avoid most of the heavy morning traffic which would all be coming into the city and you'd be heading out. Near large cities it's best to find a well-known motel chain with a brightly lit parking lot.

I only got burned once. It was pretty late in the evening because I'd been lost all that day, so I stopped at a motel on the outskirts of Kansas City. I took a ground floor unit and it turned out to be a sleazy swinging door establishment. Traffic was heavy all night. I think they rented the rooms by the hour. At first I was scared, but after an hour or so of hearing giggles and moans, I began to see the humor in the experience. I'll admit I didn't sleep much that night. I did prop a chair in front of my door and I was out of there by morning's first light.

In Oklahoma, I left the freeway and took a side trip to see an oil drilling rig up close. I don't know where I mustered the courage, but I drove right out into the oil field and stopped in front of the trailer house office. I told the fellow in charge I was a housewife from Minnesota and that I'd like to see how the oil pumps worked. You know, those big machines that look like dinosaurs nodding their heads up and down.

The crewmen not only brought me up onto the pumping platform, but they let me handle one of the levers. I have no idea what the lever controlled, but I did get a chance to get my hands greasy with raw petroleum, also known out there as "liquid gold." The foreman and several of the crew members took me to lunch at their mess trailer. They were dirty, smelled of oil and were a rough looking crew, but they were friendly, funny and really nice guys. They treated me like they would have treated their own mother.

On the freeways in Nebraska, Kansas, Oklahoma and even northern Texas, one can drive for hundreds of miles and look across the flat plains and not see a single town, only grain elevators and cattle and a thousand miles of blue sky.

I reached Dallas in the middle of October and spent one week with my friends seeing the sights of the glass city and then moved on to Arkansas. I wanted to swim in one of their hot springs, but I never found a place, so I bypassed Little Rock and headed north to Russellville to visit an old neighbor from my days in Minneapolis. They now lived in the village of Dover, Arkansas.

Both Harland and his wife Margaret had at one time been race car drivers. He had driven professionally and she drove in Powder Puff derbies. Through we had kept in touch over the years, I hadn't seen them in person for over 20 years. I was shocked. They had grown older, but damn it, so had I. We had a marvelous visit and I was so glad I had stopped to see them. I left their home feeling renewed and reconnected with my life.

After leaving Dover, I drove straight through Missouri and Iowa in about three days, stopping only to eat, sleep, and gas up. I was anxious to return home. It had been a rewarding adventure and I was proud of myself for driving almost 3,000 miles all on my own.

I felt I'd gleaned a great many life lessons in my 31 days on the road. I felt more secure in my newfound independence. I'd grown more self confident and hadn't felt lonely or afraid on the whole long trip. I knew Bernie had been in the passenger seat right beside me all the way. I don't think my children ever really understood why I needed to go on this journey, but I knew I had to do it and I've never regretted my decision.

The 13 months I spent at Bernie's bedside also taught me many important lessons about life. Those months taught me patience, compassion and the true meaning of courage and love. I watched as someone who had once been totally blind to nature's beauty gratefully become aware of the small gifts Mother Nature gives out. Like the tiny hummingbirds feeding at the nectar bottle outside his window or a shimmering raindrop as it zigzags its way down a window pane, and the glorious colors of a rainbow on the horizon after a summer storm.

The 31 days on the highway taught me that the person inside of me is not weak or fearful of the unknown. I learned she was willing to take risks and explore and enjoy the wonderful world around her. She is curious and friendly and trusting to a fault, because she came to believe people are basically honest and good, and willing to offer a helping hand. If I have harvested any wisdom from this personal journey, it is that I must always be who I really am, my own person and to follow my heart and always keep my dreams alive. But even more importantly, I learned firsthand how to face death courageously.

Backyard Garden

Spring is here again and my green thumb is itching. I took a hike out to where I used to plant my garden, but I hadn't planted a garden there for several years. It's not a good place for a garden. There are too many tall trees surrounding it and almost no sunshine can get to it, but it's really all we've got. I stood beside my plot pondering, should I put a garden in again this year or not?

The little elf on my left shoulder warned me, "Remember it's a lot of hard work."

The fairy on my right shoulder reminded me, "But it was so much fun."

Left shoulder, "Dirty work."

Right shoulder, "But lots of tomatoes."

Left side, "Sweaty work."

Right side, "But bowls of green beans."

Left side, "Long hours."

Right side, "Fresh air, fresh flowers, fresh cucumbers."

The right shoulder fairy won the argument.

I gathered my garden tools into the little, rusty two wheeled cart, pulled on my canvas work gloves and marched out to garden plot. The soil had already been tilled, so all I had to do was rake it smooth and make my rows and plant the seeds.

Over the next three months of growing season, I had a steady audience of advisers, onlookers and doubters.

Everyone stated their methods of gardening loud and clear, and voiced their own personal opinion about gardening, but no one offered to help.

Some of the suggestions and opinions:

1. How many years have you planted in this same spot? That's way too many.

2. You know you're wasting your time doing it that way.

3. You should have roto-tilled the ground much deeper.

4. Don't plant so deep, the seeds will never reach daylight.

5. Never plant before Memorial Day.

6. Should have got those seeds in earlier if you want to grow a full crop.

7. Use commercial fertilizer it gives your veggies a kick start.

8. Use only cow manure; it's the only natural fertilizer.

9. Commercial fertilizer will ruin the soil. It only makes the weeds grow.

10. Plant underground crops in the increase of the moon.

11. Plant underground crops in the decrease of the moon

12. Plant rows all north and south, they get both morning and afternoon sun.

13. Don't you know you should never plant rows north and south?

14. Why plant a garden anyway? It's cheaper to buy them at the farmer's market.

That last remark is true enough. I planted my garden as I always did and I raised a fair amount of vegetables and a multitude of beautiful flowers, and then when harvest time arrived, so did the group of advisers.

Again they gathered around my plot and commented:

1. Oh, looks pretty good.

2. Nice work.

3. So things really did grow.

4. Mind if we pick a few tomatoes?

5. May I cut a bouquet of flowers?

"Hey! Did you help me this summer? Did you do any of the work?" I asked them point blank. Their jaws dropped and they just stared at me.

"Well then, I guess the answer is NO. Have you ever read the story of the Little Red Hen? Well, read it. Maybe it will give you a clue to why I say no to you now. So move out of my way. I've got ripe tomatoes to pick."

Hugger

We have a hugger in our midst. She is a good soul and means well, but whenever you meet her on the sidewalk or the grocery store or in the back yard, she will come rushing at you, arms opened wide, grab you and proceed to crush your ribs in her embrace. Whenever I see her coming, I have a strong impulse to turn and run for my life. When she comes dashing at me, I have the feeling I am going to be gobbled up by an ogre.

I've never been comfortable hugging strangers. I like being hugged by my children and grandkids, and even good old friends. I liked being cuddled in my loved one's arms, but when people I hardly know come reaching out to hug me, I step back with my palms held out in front of me to keep them at a distance.

Hugging someone just for show or someone you don't even care about, seems phony and foolish to me. And group hugging makes me want to run the other way. A strong-gripped handshake means a hell of a lot more to me. A good handshake indicates you are sincere and your word is good.

People seemed more honest back in the good old handshaking days. Leave the hugging to old maid aunts is my advice.

The hugging lady has several other attributes besides her friendly nature. She is a patriotic citizen and you can always recognize her on the sidewalk by the red wagon. She doesn't drive, but instead carries all her groceries and other purchases in her heavily decorated Red Flyer. She has five or six American flags mounted on the wooden side rails of the wagon, which is also plastered with patriotic stickers. "Vote Republican," "Vote Democratic," "Vote YES," "Vote NO," "Go Green!"

I don't know were she stands politically and I'm not sure she does either, I think she just likes them all. Her hobby is picking up the small sticks in the yard after a storm and also the white plastic bags that blow around freely in this area. Her efforts are helpful and appreciated. After all it helps keep our neatly landscaped yard clear of litter.

I wonder if she's a throwback to the Hug-A-Tree generation.

Locked In The Garage

In the early evening of the first day of July, five of my friends from the building next door and I were relaxing in the shade on their patio, discussing plans for the Fourth of July. No one was going anywhere special that afternoon, so we decided to plan a potluck and cookout. The complex has a large gas grill for the tenants to use, so we decided to make it a grilling party. Everyone was to furnish their own preferred cut of meat, their own plate and silverware, and another dish of something to share and pass around.

The street in front of the apartments seemed extra busy. Cars were coming and going steadily in and out the parking lot. No one really paid attention when Ruby pulled her car into the parking lot and then right into her garage. No one noticed the garage door had closed.

After a few minutes Mabel asked, "Did Ruby go in already?"

We stopped talking and looked around.

"No, I didn't see her pass by."

"Me neither."

We looked at each other puzzled. Then we all heard the frantic shouting coming from the row of garages.

"She must be stuck inside." worried Phyllis, getting quickly out of her chair.

"Why doesn't she press her garage door opener?" Anne asked. "Doesn't she have a button inside her garage to open the door?"

By this time we were all standing outside her garage

door trying to calm her and calling questions and suggestion in through the closed door.

"Calm down, Ruby, we'll get the door opened, just calm down," I called in to her. "Where is your garage door remote? Do you have it with you?"

"No!" she sobbed. It's on the front seat in my car and my car doors have all locked and I must have pressed the remote accidentally. Oh God, I'll never get out of here!" She began to wail.

"Calm down Ruby, stop crying and think. Are all your car doors locked?

"Yes!"

"Are any of the windows opened far enough to reach in and unlock a door?" I asked.

"No." she answered. She had quieted down somewhat and was in a calmer state of mind.

"Listen Ruby, is it dark in there?"

"Of course it's dark in here! There's no window and the door is shut!" she shouted sarcastically. I could understand her sarcasm, so I just ignored it.

"Walk towards the door and feel along the wall for a light switch, okay?" I called in to her.

She did as she was instructed and sure enough, she found a light switch and turned it on.

"Thank you, thank you, thank you," we could hear her repeating.

"Now Ruby, look near that light switch and see if you

can see a little white button near the door frame," I called in again to her.

We waited with bated breath outside the door as Ruby searched for the little white button.

"Here it is! I found it! Here it is!"

"Press it!" we all called excitedly. She did and up rolled the door.

We were all holding our breath and at the first sight of Ruby, we burst into laughter. There stood Ruby Bennett, the always perfectly groomed Ruby Bennett, looking like a bedraggled old raccoon. Her tears had washed her mascara from around her eyes and it was running down her cheeks and mixing with her make-up. Ruby's always neatly styled hairdo now stuck straight out like a wild cactus plant.

We were all laughing hilariously when she suddenly burst into more tears.

"I could have died in there. And you all think it's funny."

I opened my arms to her and the poor frightened little lady fell into them. "Oh Ruby, we didn't think your ordeal was funny, it's just your make-up. You always have it so perfect and now it's a mess and it's just such a shock to see you like that."

"Come on," coaxed Mabel. "Let's go inside. You can wash up and redo your face and then we'll come out and drink our lemonade. And we will all forget about this little escapade."

"Oh yeah, like you girls will ever forget it. I know you ladies, you'll never forget about this, nor will you ever let me forget about it." But she began to laugh good-naturedly.

What Life Does

This is what life does:

Life encourages you to take risks if you want to get ahead,
but it never allows you to preview the outcome.

Life is like a donkey cart driver dangling the carrot of success
just out of your reach, but like the villain,
when you're about to grasp it, it jerks the bait away.

Life is an illusionist and when you think you've got its mystery
figured out, it changes direction,
and becomes completely foreign to you again.

And then after years of dieting and sit-ups and wrinkle creams,
gravity steps into life uninvited,
and all your hard work is pulled downward.

Is there a solution to this dilemma?
Can we hold life at bay?

I'm afraid not, life is unstoppable;
it continues its march forward relentlessly.

So how can we save ourselves
from all of life's useless frustrations?

Only by honoring Mother Nature's remedy,
"Go with the flow."

Love Sounds

Have you ever stopped to think about what sounds you really love? Like a baby's giggle or a cat purring on your lap or the wind blowing through the tops of pine trees. I've always delighted in listening to the rumbling of far off thunder and then I wait in anticipation as the storm approaches. I love to hear the thunder, see the lightning and feel the wind. Some people are frightened by storms, but I am invigorated by them and it fills me with energy and excitement. I love the rhythm of the rain drumming on the rooftop and the patter of raindrops on the window panes.

I'm lulled into relaxation at night by the symphony of the crickets and frogs in the marsh across the street and sometimes I can hear the little hoot owl in the trees behind my building. Later at night, if I can't sleep, I listen to the continuous humming of the tires on the big eighteen wheelers as they spin over the concrete on the freeway half a mile away.

Sounds are everywhere, constantly, even when you think the world is completely still. Try sitting alone in the quietest place you can find and just close your eyes and listen. At first it seems there are no sounds at all, but then you hear a dry leaf flutter on the ground and a bee buzzing close by. Then a fly passes and a car horn honks at a far distance. A phone is ringing somewhere, a car passes by, the wind chimes tinkle, and you recognize children's muffled laughter and a couple talking quietly as they walk past on the sidewalk. Far off you can hear an emergency vehicle's siren.

You'll hear bird calls you never noticed before. A robin calling for rain. Crows cawing and morning doves cooing. You can hear the "chic-a-dee-dee-dee" of the little black masked birds, the chirping of the brown sparrows and a blue jay scolding in a nearby treetop. There is even a little wren singing in the pine tree and a hummingbird whose wings make a whirling sound while it hovers above a petunia blossom. A butterfly silently flutters past. This sheltered refuge is by no means idle; it's alive with life and busy with activity.

Sometimes when I am sitting in these quietly peaceful surroundings with my eyes closed, I let my mind drift back to the years I lived a more active life in the interior of the beautiful Black Hills of South Dakota. I relished the nights I could hear wolves howl, elk bugle and coyotes yipping while on their night chase. I still long to hear the eagles scream as they soar effortlessly on the thermal currents high above the treetops. Or to hear the braying of the wild burro in Custer State Park when they are begging for handouts from the tourists passing by in their cars. I would love one more chance to feel the ground tremble and hear the thunder of a hundred buffalo hooves pounding the earth as the confined herd of the great beasts take off on an afternoon run through the park's valleys.

But those days are long gone and I'm now at home in Minnesota living the quiet life. I still miss the tall ponderosa pines and the sheer rock cliffs and evenings outside with no mosquitoes. But I'm back on home ground, back to where I can once again witness spectacular summer storms. I'll love the flash of lightning and I'll glory in every rumble of thunder and rejoice in the sound of the rain pounding on my roof, as I cuddle beneath my soft flannel sheets.

Bathtub Treat

It was a scorcher today and Laura's air conditioner wasn't working up to par. She looked forward to dunking herself right up to her chin in a bathtub filled of tepid water.

After watching the six o'clock news she locked her hall door. She went into the bathroom, put the stopper in the bathtub drain and turned on the cold water. She put her hand under the running cold water and it felt wonderful, but she didn't want the water in the tub to be that cold, so she adjusted the temperature of the bath water by adding a slow stream of hot water to heat it. When she was sure it was mixing well she went into her bedroom and stripped off all her damp, sweaty clothes to ready herself for her bathtub treat.

The phone stared ringing. "Who the heck is that," she wondered. "Nobody I know ever calls me at this time of day. It might be something important so I'd better answer it."

Laura peeked out into the living room to make sure the drapes were closed before she hurried to the phone. She wasn't the kind of woman who ran around her apartment in the nude. "Hello. Who is this?" she asked.

"It's me, your sister Mary, I'm calling from Chicago. What are you doing tomorrow? Billy and I are driving into the Twin Cities and I'd like to come see you."

"Oh Mary, that would be wonderful." Laura sat down on the couch in her birthday suit and the two sisters began to visit in earnest.

A half hour passed and Clara, who lived in the apartment below Laura began to notice a water mark staining her ceiling. Soon it was more than a stain. Water began dripping down the kitchen wall and the bathroom ceiling began to sag.

"Oh my God a water pipe has broken. I'll have to call Harold right quick!" Clara grabbed the phone and dialed the custodian. "Harold, Harold, come quick! This is Clara Carlson in apartment 109 and a water pipe must have broken in the ceiling. My apartment is flooding! Hurry, hurry!" Clara slammed down the receiver just as the bathroom ceiling ripped open with a gush of water spraying the walls. "Oh Harold, hurry," prayed Clara.

Harold didn't bother to knock. He burst into the apartment just as the ceiling gave way. "Ye Gods, the water is coming from the bathroom upstairs. Laura must have left her water running."

Harold turned on his heels and dashed up the stairs to unit 209 and started pounding frantically on the locked door. He pulled out his pass key and unlocked the door and threw it opened. Laura leaped from the couch, dropped her phone and stood frozen to the spot, buck naked. Harold, a confirmed bachelor, nearly fainted and his eyes bulged out. Clara stood in Laura's doorway, soaking wet and fuming mad.

The water was quickly turned off. A wet-vac sucked up the flood of water from the floor and a fan worked hard to dry it, but poor Harold's nerves were shot.

Things did turn out okay for the trio. Clara's damaged ceiling was repaired with new sheetrock and carpet, plus the whole apartment was repainted. Laura got a serious reprimand, a new bathroom floor, a walk-in shower instead of a tub and an embarrassment she may never recover from.

And Harold? Well, he received an unusual education and the thrill of his lifetime.

Think You're Bored?

Oh, so you think you're bored and you'd like to find some excitement. Well, you won't find adventure just sitting around watching soap operas or a movie on Netflix. Real life adventure seldom comes knocking at your door, you actually have to get up out of your comfort zone and look for it. Sometimes you can find it just around the corner or maybe just down the block. It could be hiding behind any closed door or maybe inside an open one.

Adventure isn't only found at spectacular events, it can be found in quiet and simple places, like your front patio or the backyard. You might find it reading a good book on a rainy day or even while you're picking green beans in your garden or baking chocolate chip cookies for your grandkids. Just leave yourself open to possibilities. Sometimes just saying hello to a person you've never met before will open up a door to adventure.

Try letting someone with a grocery cart fuller than yours get ahead of you in the check-out line. Just smile at them and say: "You may go ahead of me." They may be so grateful they'll start up a conversation, and presto, a new friend. Which may lead to the possibility of a new adventure.

I know, that is a roundabout way to get there. I have a quicker way. Take a day trip on a senior bus to anywhere. There will be other seniors on that bus looking for new friends, too.

Do volunteer work at your local hospital or senior center. Take a community ed class. Help out at a local day care center. If that's not your thing, go with a group on a longer bus or train tour. See the U.S.A., as the old Dinah Shore song says. What I'm trying to say is meet new people. Actually go out of your way to bring new people into your life and don't be afraid to ask others what they do to entertain themselves and then adopt and improvise. The main objective here is to get you up on your feet and out of your apartment doing something different.

The best adventure I ever had was on an Elderhostel tour. It was a 12 day covered wagon trip through the Black Hills in South Dakota. On a smaller scale, I had another good adventure by simply finding a wonderful book at my local library. There have been hundreds of memorable events I can recall and I like to think of them all as adventures.

I Start Writing

The long solitary trip I'd taken after my husband passed away was rewarding and gratifying, but the lonely endless winter that followed was almost unbearable. I found myself completely alone for the first time in my life.

I wasn't physically frightened of being alone, after all my husband had been away every weekday working in the city the first years we'd lived on the farm. I wasn't afraid of bodily harm. It was the knowledge of knowing I was out here alone and I would have to survive on my own wits.

I wasn't totally convinced that I could do it, but I knew I had to. I started new hobbies. I took up knitting, but one can only use so many scarves. I crocheted several granny square afghans and I taught myself to make macramé plant hangers, but one can only use so many of them as well.

One day I sat down in front of the picture windows and stared out at the beauty of the open, snow-covered fields, and the birds at the feeders. I began to see it all as Bernie must have viewed it. I became inspired and began writing poetry about nature and then moved on to children's stories in rhyme. I started writing about the funny things that happen on a farm. Dog stories and cow stories and even stories about my silly crested white goose named Soda Quacker. I discovered writing was my passion and also my salvation. I never tried to publish any of these stories, I only considered them my personal therapy.

Rim Of The World

I sat on the rim of the world today
and watched creation pass my way.
The dance of the butterfly, the flight of a bird,
the voice of the creek I even heard.

White clouds drifted lazily over my head,
"This earth is magnificent" the breeze gently said.
Shy deer ventured near me, a trout jumped below,
The leather backed snapper made her way, sure but slow.

I sighed ever so softly, but the wood duck took heed,
And the black bird took flight from the bend in the reed.
A bumble bee buzzing, a cricket, a frog,
A slender green snake in the sun on a log.

The branches enfold me, the creek bed's below
Reflecting the dazzle of leaves all aglow.
If all of God's children could just someday see
This glorious world, from this branch, in this tree.

Story Time

I have almost given up hope of ever having any of the residents share their personal stories. Everyone here is so secretive about their past. I'm beginning to doubt that any of them ever did anything in their earlier years. It seems no one will talk about their good old days. I wondered why. Everywhere else I'd ever lived friends readily talked about their youth and their early years of marriage and their babies and their first jobs.

I know there are great experiences tucked away in the memories of the residents who dwell in this complex. There has to be, because on average most of the occupants here are in their 70s and 80s, so they would have witnessed the many changes this country has passed through in the past century. So much has happened.

One evening while playing a card game called "hand and foot" my card partner for this evening's game suddenly said, "It makes me so damn mad and sad too, when I see coaches, and parents lighting into a kid for not performing to their idea of absolute perfection. God, don't they realize the kid is trying to do the best she can?"

There was fire In her eyes and her fist was clenched.

"Hey Ruthie, what brought that on?" I asked.

"I've been watching the gymnastic teams at the games in London and I couldn't help notice how rough the coaches are on the kid if she doesn't flip just right or lands a little wobbly," Ruthie said. "It makes me think of when I was a kid and how tough my ma was on me if I missed a step or dropped a baton. She'd make me practice an extra two hours every day for the next full week. I already had to spend five hours a day in music classes. Either dance classes or voice classes or acrobatic classes or whatever."

"Gosh, Ruthie, were you a performer when you were a kid?" I asked.

"Yes," she answered with sad blue eyes and a tear balancing on her eyelid. "It was the Shirley Temple era, and my ma had convinced my dad that I had a lot of talent and that I could become famous like Shirley and make them all rich.'

"I did have a little talent, but not to that extent," she continued. "My mother wanted to live her dream of being on the stage through me. So, from the time I was four until I was fifteen, I'd spent most of my days in rehearsal studios. Dance classes and voice classes, I even had to learn to play my dad's big accordion. It was almost as big and heavy as me, when I first learned to play it." She laughed a little as she remembered trying to lug the big squeeze box onto the stage.

"My mother's whole life was wrapped up in making my life her musical career. Our family was not wealthy, but my mother hired an agent to handle bookings. She spent every dime she could scrounge up to further my career. She so wanted me to make her famous. Then Ma and the agent formed a trio of other talented youngsters to perform with me. I sang and danced and played the accordion, while the others served as back-up singers. They named our group 'Baby Ruthie and The All Stars.'"

"Where did you go to school?" asked Ruby. We had stopped playing cards now and were all listening intently to Ruthie's story.

"I never got to go to public school when I was school age. I never had a chance to make real friends. I missed out on my whole childhood," she said bitterly. "That's why it makes me so mad when I see programs on TV showing mothers making their poor little girls act like grown-up models or movie stars. I say, let those kids be kids."

"Did you make a lot of money?" somebody asked.

"I don't know. I never got any of it. It all went to my mother and the agent. My share, they told me, went to buy new costumes because I was growing too fast."

"How long did you continue to perform?" I asked.

"Well, my father and my brother never approved of my having to entertain in the sleazy nightspots and dinner clubs in the Twin Cities and surrounding areas. This was in the late 1930s. Some of the spots would get pretty rowdy late at night with all the booze being passed under the table. Then one night, when I was getting ready to leave for my evening gig, my brother Ralph stepped forward and told my mother, "This is enough. Ruthie is too nice a girl to be forced to dance her whole youth away in those damn speakeasies. You and your flunky agent have made enough money off her already. Let her have a life."

At that announcement, a cheer went up from all of us in the card room. We all hugged Ruthie and congratulated her. The card game resumed.

Later, Ruth told me there had been a violent quarrel that night at her home and her entertainment obligations ended abruptly. She enrolled in a Minneapolis high school and spent the next four years living as a normal teenager. School girl crushes, puppy love and all the rest. She never mentioned her mother again, so I don't know how that part of her life turned out. She told me she enjoyed her high school years and she graduated in the upper quarter of her class.

She didn't go into detail about the next years of her life,

87

but she told me she worked as a typesetter for a Minneapolis newspaper company for many years. Ruthie said she had a long and happy marriage and several children--and I'll bet she let them all be kids in their childhood years.

I've known Ruthie for several years and I never expected this sort of story coming from her. I'd always thought of her as a rather shy and withdrawn person. But now she comes across as an outgoing personality, open and fun-loving.

I only wish I could peek into a few more of our residents' secret lives. I'll bet some of their stories could fill a complete book of surprises.

Get Those Stories Out

I'm going to try a whole new method of getting stories out of these reluctant hermits. I'll try the Story Time approach. We did this in a women's group back in South Dakota and it drew all the members into the experience.

We would pick a subject related to our project of the month and then everyone in the group would tell a short story about an experience connected with the subject we were discussing. The idea worked well back then, but would it work with this bunch of stick-in-the-muds?

I printed a notice in BOLD LETTERS and taped it to the front door using several long strips of scotch tape to make sure the note stayed straight and stuck to the door. The notice stated the day of the gathering, the time we would meet, and the reason for the meeting. (It also mentioned there would be FREE COFFEE and DONUTS). I explained the stories should be short, but they did not have to be completely accurate. I stressed that stretching the truth a bit is totally allowable in story telling. But we did not want to hear stories that were gruesome or too personal. Funny stories are always good. So are animal stories and baby stories.

I set the Story Time to be held in Middle Manor's Community Room the first and third Thursday of each month. The first gathering would be next Thursday afternoon at 1:30. I hoped for the best. I also wrote a poem and printed enough copies to tape one on every resident's door on the morning of the first meeting date, just as a reminder. Folks our age do forget easily.

> Sometimes I think my personal mood
> Depends upon the weather,
> Come stormy days or cloudy days
> My moods don't seem much better.

But when a lovely day appears
My gloomy feelings fade

Then in my view or on my path
A sunbeam will be laid.

Our viewpoint then must brighter be
Or life will seem so hollow,
'Cause when we walk along our path
Our attitude will follow.

We've got to keep our old eyes sharp
And grasp the joys of now,
Or we'll just sit and vegetate
It's up to us somehow.

Our bodies might not perfect be,
But still a breath we're taking
We've got to grasp at life right now
In morning we're still waking.

So please embrace your here and now
With gratitude be caring,
SO WILL YOU COME AND SIT WITH ME
YOUR JOYS IN LIFE BE SHARING?

To my absolute astonishment twelve people showed up. I announced, before the group had settled down, the subject of our stories today would be "An Animal in Your Life." After much coaxing, three ladies agreed to share their stories. Two of the stories were only two liners, but at least they tried.

Jessie: "I had to milk old Bess every morning and evening. One morning she kicked over the pail of milk and my ma got real mad." Jessie blushed and sat down.

"Very good Jessie, and thank you for sharing."

Mavis: "We lived in the city and our dog Jeff once bit

the mailman. My dad gave him away to a farmer and the farmer liked Jeff a lot because he was good with the cows and the farmer's kids"

"That was good too, Mavis. Thanks."

Kate: "My story is called Jug Head."

Jug Head

Jug Head was one of the three half-Airedale puppies I had decided to keep. Molly, our purebred female Airedale had surprised us with a litter of thirteen half-Golden Lab puppies on a very cold September night. They had all been born under our camper trailer. I had to crawl on my belly to get them all out from under the trailer. I picked out three pups to keep, but I had to have the remaining ten puppies put to sleep, because Molly would or could not nurse them all. Ten puppies were just too many to try to bottle feed by hand.

One of the puppies I kept I named Scooter. He had all the perfect body features of a purebred Airedale, except he was completely golden in color. Another pup was named Wobbles, because he swayed back and forth when he walked. He reminded me of a drunken sailor. The third one was named Jug Head. Both Wobbles and Jug Head were marked like genuine Airedales. I had all three of their tails docked and the dew claws removed, planning to give all three of them to friends of mine. I named Scooter because of the way he dashed from one place to another always in a hurry. Jug Head got his name in a totally unique way.

We had about six calico cats and together they ate a lot of dry cat food, so I would buy it in 100 lb. bags from the feed store. To keep the cat food fresh, I would store it in large plastic three gallon jugs. I would fill the jugs with the dry cat food, cover them tightly, and store them on the back porch.

Our side yard runs along the edge of the south bank of Willow Creek and there is about a six foot drop down to the fast running water. The water was flowing swiftly at this time of year. I was busy working in my garden and I stopped to rest. I was about fifty feet from the creek when I heard a muffled, squeaky bark. I looked around and saw only two pups standing in the yard staring at the creek. This was odd because the three puppies were always together. They ate together, slept together and always played together, side by side. Seeing just the two of them alone was unusual and so I thought I'd better investigate.

I dropped my hoe and followed the sound of the muffled grunts and barks, and then I saw the third puppy teetering on the very edge of the cliff above the water. The poor little thing couldn't see were he was going because there was a plastic jug stuck over his head. I rushed to grab him before he could tumble over the edge. If he had fallen at that spot the jug would have filled up with water and he would have drowned.

The puppies must have found one jar of cat food with a loose cover, tipped it over, and ate all the contents. Little Jug Head, being the smallest of the three, must have been the last to eat out of the jug and he wanted to get every last morsel. In doing so, he got his head stuck in the jug and he couldn't get it off. Of course the moral to this story is: That's what happens when you're greedy."

Christmas To Remember

I was happy to see so many of the residents show up for the storytelling, but they didn't all enjoy it I guess, because two of them fell asleep and three of them left when we ran out of cookies.

The second gathering of the storytelling group was somewhat smaller. The three ladies who had shared last time showed up again and that was encouraging. The two men that had eaten all the cookies last time were there again, only this time they brought along several plastic Ziploc bags to take home some of the treats. They drank two cups of coffee each, filled their plastic bags and left. Oh well.

Our subject the second week is to be about "The Christmas You Will Always Remember."

Lilly is new to our building and the smallest person I'd ever met. She probably doesn't stand over four feet six inches and is perhaps about 85 years old, but she seems to be a pistol. She's not the least bit shy and it's easy to tell she's going to be a fun person to have around.

Lilly: "I have a Christmas Story from way back when I was just a sprout. It was at the very beginning of the Great Depression and my folks were both out of work. My sister who was nine years older than me and very wise, told me we would not be getting any presents this year because Santa Claus was just as poor as we were. This was very bad news. After all, didn't he live in the North Pole and own his own toy factory? Were all the elves out of work, too? Were there dust storms even way up in the snow-covered North Pole?

Like all kids, I always looked forward to Christmas and then my birthday, three days later. I wondered if we would still be going to church on Christmas Eve, because after the program about Jesus being born in a stable, the preacher's wife would always hand out a brown paper bag with an orange and peanuts and hard candy to all the kids who had attended the service.

Last year, we had a tree in our living room and when we got home from church I found a present under it for me, but my sister said there wouldn't be any this year 'cause we don't have a tree. Grandpa didn't go to church with us, he said it was too cold and he'd rather stay home where it's warm.

It had snowed yesterday and all the yards were sparkling like crystal sugar in the moonlight. I could see the stars twinkling clearly in the inky black sky and they reminded me of the pictures of diamond rings in black satin boxes in the Sears catalog.

We had to walk eight blocks to our house, but the night was so beautiful I somehow felt happy in spite of the fact there would be no gifts this year. I clutched the brown bag with the orange and peanuts even more tightly.

When we were almost home, I ran ahead and dashed into the house intending to show Grandpa what I'd gotten in the paper bag. I stopped short inside the front door, my eyes popping wide opened. There stood a Christmas tree. It was unlike any other Christmas tree I'd ever seen. It was short and squat and reddish green with branches as sharp as needles. There were no decorations on it, but it was a tree. I knew now for sure that Santa will be coming to our house tonight, we had a tree.

Grandpa had cut the tree from along the railroad tracks and his face and hand were scratched from the sharp needles of the cedar tree. The branches were so prickly we couldn't even get close enough to put any trim on it.

Mother just laughed and suggested we stand way back and toss little pieces of colored yarn onto the branches. "It will be safer that way," she said. It made the little tree look happy and bright and cheery.

Following our regular Christmas tradition, Mom made cocoa and toast and we all sang carols until it was my bedtime. I was so excited about the coming night, I had a hard time falling asleep. Would Santa like our different-looking tree? It really wasn't like a Christmas Tree at all. But Mama said the little tree felt really honored to be serving as a stand-in Christmas tree for people that couldn't afford a real Christmas tree. I put two cookies on a plate for Santa and a bowl of sauerkraut for his reindeer. To encourage me to eat sauerkraut, Grandpa always told me it was the reindeer's favorite treat. I truly doubted that.

I was hoping to hear Santa's sleigh on the rooftop, but I must have fallen asleep, because when I opened my eyes, it was morning. I jumped out of bed and dashed down the steps and there a little ways away from the prickly little tree sat our presents. Santa Claus did come! He didn't care that our little tree was "different."

Mama and Daddy were already up and smiling broadly, their eyes dancing. Grandpa and my sister Lois were still asleep.

"Can I open them now? I begged.

"Of course you can, they're yours." Mama smiled at me.

"What do you think he made for you this year?" asked Daddy.

I tore off the wrapping paper. (It looked just like the

Christmas paper they used at the grocery store.) I couldn't believe my eyes. A whole box full of new doll clothes. There were dresses and nighties and panties and even a belted coat. There was a new blanket and pillow just dolly size.

"Oh Mama, Santa knew just what I wanted!" I squealed with delight. I quickly tore opened the second box.

"Mama, Daddy! Look! A doll cradle, just Betsy's size and look, the pillow and blanket fits just right! Oh, I love them all!"

Later in the morning, when Grandpa and Daddy opened their gifts from Santa, they both received a new winter shirt. Both shirts were tan flannel just like Betsy's belted coat. "Mrs. Santa must have gotten a really good buy on tan flannel this year," I thought to myself, "and Betsy's two dresses have the same print as my sister Lois's two new blouses, now isn't that nice?" I concluded.

My birthday is three days after Christmas and Daddy had made me two little wooden chairs just alike. He painted them both red. One chair was my size and the other one was Betsy's size."

That concluded Lilly's Christmas Story, but she did add one more sentence: "It was the most wonderful holiday I'd ever had, and it was my 'Christmas to Remember.'"

Santa's Helpers

Do you believe in Santa Claus?
Why of course you do!
But don't you ever wonder how he keeps his eye on you?
How can Santa watch all children, every single one?
Now you might think that it's a job that simply can't be done. Santa
has a group of helpers and they work the whole year through.
I will tell you how he found them and exactly what they do.

He was sitting at his work bench, wondering who he'd try,
Bunnies work at Easter, so he'd have to pass them by.
Some apartments can't have puppies so they won't do the job.
Cats are always napping and turtles like to bob.
Now birds would do quite nicely, but they must stay outside,
And guinea pigs and hamsters always want to hide.
He could use ponies in the country or cows that gently moo,
Or cackling hens and roosters, but what would city children do?
Now youngsters in the city might keep goldfish in a jar,
Or a parrot in a painted cage, but they can't watch too far.

Santa sat all night just thinking, and then to his surprise,
From a pile of old wood shavings flashed a pair of twinkling eyes.
"Ho ho! Now there's my answer!" shouted Santa with delight,
But the furry little creature scampered off the bench in fright.

Santa asked the little gray mouse and all his family too,
To be his Christmas helpers and this is what they do:
They can peek from every corner and they watch, so you be good,
'Cause at Christmas they'll tell Santa if you've acted like you should.
You can tell a Christmas helper by his small red stocking hat,
This makes him an official helper and they're very proud of that.
So when Santa comes to your house and gray mouse reports on you,
I hope your stocking's stuffed with toys and love and laughter, too.

Ragweed Playhouse

Our story hour continued for a few more months, but interest dwindled. It appeared the residents were actually interested in hearing the other people's stories, but too few were willing to share their treasured experiences.

To be a success, story hour would have to have both willing listeners and generous storytellers and I'm sorry to say, after a few months we ran out of both.

Maybe my cookies had grown stale or the coffee got too strong, I'll never know. There was one more subject that brought out an interesting story, it was "My Favorite Playmate" and it was shared by my friend Phyllis.

Phyllis: "My folks were dirt poor farmers during the depression years of the 1930s. We lived on a pig farm in central South Dakota. But like every other farmer during that time, we were devastated by the brutal drought and terrible dust storms. For several years, our family, consisting of my mother and father and my two grandmothers, one from each side of the family, lived with us, and we lived a hand-to-mouth existence. Our farm at one time had been fertile soil, raising hundreds of acres of corn and was a productive pig farm. But Mother Nature and the failure of the country's banks changed all that.

Our family was now bankrupt, and the property no longer belonged to us. We stayed on the farm anyway, because here at least we were able to grow our own food. Our well was still good and had not gone dry like many others, so we were really better off than the folks who lived in the cities.

I was only five years old, so of course I did not realize we were so poor. I had never had to go without at least a meager meal, so I was never really hungry. I was an only child and had to learn to play by myself, although I never felt like I was playing alone, because I had so many make-believe playmates. My favorite place to play was in the old abandoned pig yards. Here the ragweed plants grew from six to eight feet tall.

My grandmothers both said it was not a healthy place for a youngster to play, but Ma said she thought it was fine, and beside, she said, she always knew where to find me.

It was a perfect place to pretend. Here I could cut down, with the use of an old tin snip, several stalks of ragweed and pretend the open space was my castle or it could be the deck of a pirate ship, but mostly I just pretended it was a plain house with many, many rooms. I would push my way through the thick canes of the giant plants and step off the area I'd choose for each of my pretend rooms. Usually I'd want three rooms: a kitchen, a living room and a bedroom. Each room would be about five feet square. I would cut down or pull up the plants growing in my marked-off area and then carefully remove the root ends and all the velvety leaves. I'd then lay the large, soft leaves neatly on the bare dirt floor to be used as scatter rugs. I'd cut off the tangled root ends and strip the plant's stem clean. The hardest part of this project was weaving the now stripped plant stems between the heavy stalks of the still growing plants, to indicate the location of my pretend walls.

Everything went smoothly as long as the weather stayed dry, and since there was a drought at this time it seldom rained. There was, of course, no roof over my well-planned apartment, and so, when it did rain, the whole thing turned into a smelly, muddy mess. It was, after all, an old pig yard. But not to worry, because when the ground dried out again, I'd just move my whole outfit to a new location and start over. I never ran out of building material, because the old pig yard was over an acre of giant ragweed plants.

99

My playhouse furniture consisted of two small nail kegs turned upside down, to be used as chairs. I had one orange crate laid on its side. This was my table. The second one was standing upright and was used for a cupboard. A rusty milk can, turned bottom end up, was a make-believe stove top and I had a whole cupboard full of mama's old junk pots and pans and dishes. I used all the leftover leaves and the soft stem tops to pad my bed, which was a piece of corrugated tin heaped with velvety leaves, in my make-believe bedroom. I also used the sheet of tin to transport all my furnishings when it was time to move on to a new location.

When I played alone I could pretend anything I chose to act out. I could be a pioneer woman in a sod house or a queen in a stone castle with a moat running around it. There was no end to where I could transport myself in my make-believe world.

I never felt underprivileged or lonely. I was a loner then and I still am. I was my own best playmate, because I have always felt okay with my own company.

A funny thought has occurred to me lately and I have to laugh out loud when I think of it. I can't imagine any of my grandchildren sitting on an upside down nail keg in a ragweed playhouse, punching away on their laptops or iPads in a smelly old pig yard with the bare sky overhead, and actually being outside in the open air. They would be completely baffled. And never know all the fun they'd been missing.

Eating My Words

Well, I'm grateful there are only a few calories in eating my own words. I'm going to have to eat quite a large serving of some of my own observations I'd written about several stories back. It was when I was ranting on about the lack of medical care in the hospitals nowadays. I'll have to retract many of those complaints, because an occasion arose that put a whole new perspective on my point of view.

I discovered a medical problem I had been dealing with for quite a long while had become more serious than I'd realized. I called my primary doctor's clinic expecting to be given the run around again, but a real person answered the phone on the third ring. I asked for an appointment to see my doctor and they set it for the very next day. I arrived at my appointment on time and a nurse escorted me into the examining room within ten minutes.

Holy cow! I couldn't believe this, here I am in the doctor's examining room and I only left home a half hour ago. We discussed my problem at length and she arranged an appointment for me to speak to a surgeon the next day. Three days later I was in surgery having my hemorrhoid problem corrected and here I am, one day later, back home again. Why had I procrastinated so long? Was I afraid of the doctors? Am I so old fashioned, that I was embarrassed to speak to a doctor about my condition?

Well, I'm sure glad I did, because though I'm still a bit uncomfortable today my mood is 100 percent better and I have confidence that sitting will soon be 100 percent more comfortable as well.

I guess the point I want to make is this. My hospital experience this time came off without a hitch. Everything went along smoothly, which leads me to believe that the experiences one has in this type of situation, either good or bad, might well be brought on by one's own attitude and expectations.

I've found a doctor I really like and have confidence in her. I trusted the word of the surgeon she recommended and I discovered the rest of the staff was knowledgeable and very professional. All in all, I must admit this hospital experience turned out to be far better than I had expected.

Do You Remember?

Do you remember when:

1. Pharmacies only sold prescription medicines?

2. Drugstores sold ice cream sodas?

3. $2.50 worth of gas would fill the whole tank of the old Model A Ford?

4. Pillows were filled with feathers instead of foam?

5. One could check out the new styles in the seasonal Sears catalog?

6. Only the poor kids wore tennis shoes--the rich kids had leather oxfords?

7. Hamburgers at the local fairs actually contained ground beef?

8. School kids wrote on paper tablets with lead pencils?

9. Telephones were connected to the wall with a black cord?

10. Kids felt going to Grandma's house was a treat instead of a punishment?

11. We got most of our news from the morning paper instead of TV or a handheld gadget?

12. Kids were allowed to play outside barefoot and run around in rainstorms?

13. The Tooth Fairy only had to pay ten cents for a tooth?

14. Kids believed in Santa Claus until around fifth grade?

15. Halloween was a kid's holiday?

Trick or Treat

Back in the day, on Halloween, kids could safely run from door to door in their neighborhoods and gather candy in pillowcases. Most of them were made up to look like hobos or gypsies and their folks didn't have to spend a fortune on fancy costumes. When the little goblins' bags were filled, they'd run home, dump the loot on the living room floor and charge out again for a second round. Mom and Dad would then pick out their favorite candies and hide them for their own treats later on.

Of course, the kids would eat so many goodies on their rounds that they would be sick for the next day or two, but wasn't it fun!? But now some cruel and heartless adults have spoiled this holiday for the kids, making "Trick or Treat" too dangerous, wild and worrisome for the children to enjoy their spooky and glorious Kids Night Out experience.

A New Chapter In Life

In the late spring of 1984 when I was already 55 years old, my life took a complete 90-degree turn. Life became interesting again, as a new chapter in my life opened up. I began keeping an annual journal of all my new experiences.

It had rained steadily throughout April and I knew full well the 12-acre field of alfalfa, which ran parallel to the county road, would be wet and soggy, but I decided to go for a ride anyway. I would keep Star, my 20-year-old palomino mare on the solid gravel driveway along the north edge of the field. I was sure her year-old colt, Comet, would stay close behind his mother and not get into any kind of trouble. But like any curious youngster, as soon as he realized he was loose and out of the corral, he took off galloping across the muddy field and immediately found himself stuck in the soggy gumbo. He struggled and fell to his knees and began screaming, as horses can do. Star panicked and headed for her downed offspring. The wet ground sucked at her hooves and she stumbled, throwing me over her head and face down in the mucky field. Star didn't fall and somehow managed to keep her balance. I hit the ground hard and lay there stunned for several minutes.

Finally I was able to roll over onto my back and take inventory of my injures. The ground, being so wet, was fairly soft. I decided nothing was broken, so I struggled to my feet. I was covered with mud and field debris and my eyes were blurry. I reached up to wipe the dirt out of my eyes only to realize it wasn't mud, it was blood. Apparently I'd cut a gash in my forehead. When my sight cleared I could see Star and Comet had made it out of the field and were now on the county road, but instead of heading back towards the farm, they were running west towards the river.

I tried to whistle to Star. She usually responded to my whistle, but my lips were cut and I couldn't make a sound. I knew trying to catch them now would be futile in my condition, so I concentrated on dragging myself back to the farmhouse.

I called the sheriff's department to report my missing horses as soon as I'd cleaned myself up. The neighbors all knew my horses, so I was sure someone would corral them and call me later in the day.

Two days passed and no calls. On the third day Star came home by herself, looking a little worse for the wear, but not hurt in any way. But where the hell was Comet? He was so dependent on his mother I was afraid he must be down somewhere. Late that afternoon an old beat up Chevy Silverado pickup truck turned into my driveway. Behind it, being towed unwillingly, was my mud-covered white colt. His halter was twisted to one side and was covering his left eye and he had his knees locked stubbornly and was fighting the lead rope. His one blue eye was wild and angry, but he was tied securely to the battered blue tailgate.

This was my introduction to the adventures I would experience the next 25 years. The man who brought Comet home that fateful day was destined to become an important character in the future chapters of my life.

He certainly was not my knight in shining armor, but he was the tall, handsome cowboy in tight jeans that I'd always dreamed about. Within eight months, he and his two teen-aged children had moved into my home with me. The daughter was immediately a problem. She was extremely jealous of her father's attention, having been the primary female in his life for most of her 16 years. The son, age 12, was completely different. He'd never had a mother figure and he seemed to thrive in this family setting. He was a willing worker and was always a great help to me on the farm. I soon became very fond of him and I still am.

After a year or so of raising beef cattle, I discover I had a little gravel in one of the hills on my farm, and so upon Mike's advice, I bought two gravel trucks. We became partners in a trucking company, but within two years the business folded and I had to sell the trucks at a loss. I was emotionally devastated, but not financially crushed. I'd managed to save some of our meager profits.

The next summer, I attended a business seminar at Carleton College and treated myself to my first therapeutic massage. I was so impressed, I decided this was a profession I wanted to learn, so upon my return to the Twin Cities, I enrolled in the Minneapolis School of Massage Therapy at the age of 58. I was the oldest student they had ever enrolled in this class. I doubled up on the courses and was certified and licensed in less than a year. In November 1989, I began my new career. I opened my own salon and worked in the field of therapeutic massage, facial massage, and reflexology for the next 16 years.

I am a gypsy at heart and over the next two decades I moved around the Midwest and experienced my share of ups and downs. Most of my adventures have been positive, but in the negative situations, I have always landed on my feet. Now at the ripe old age of 83, I've decided to take inventory of myself, and I've come to the conclusion my life has been full and exciting and I would not exchange it for any other.

In 1991, I traveled with an Elderhostel group for 12 days on a covered wagon tour through the interior of the beautiful Black Hills. I fell in love with the area and within two months of returning to Minnesota, I convinced Mike we should move to the hills of South Dakota. And so, in the autumn of 1991, when I was just about to turn 62, I bought a lovely house high on a hill on the south edge of the town of Custer, South Dakota and opened my first massage therapy wellness clinic in that city.

We lived and worked in this region for the next five years. But then my gypsy feet began to itch again and I sold my business at a profit and bought an extended cab diesel pickup truck with a 28-foot fifth wheel camper attached. I packed up my dog Mandy, my cat Calico, my friend Mike, and at 67, took off for the open road.

For the next two years we traveled throughout the western and northwestern states. But after a while, I realized I needed to put down roots somewhere. Due to some medical problems in Mike's family, we headed back to Minnesota, where I bought a small hobby farm two miles north of Sandstone. We also purchased a registered quarter horse mare and had her bred to a beautifully marked paint stallion. We were striving to produce a distinctively marked paint foal, but we never came close to achieving that goal.

To financially support this dream, we boarded and trained saddle horses for riding. But after a few years of hard work and several disappointments, Mike lost interest in the horse business, so we sold the horses and the farm. I packed up my dog and cat and moved back to Custer. I bought back my former salon and reopened the wellness center.

Custer is a tourist town and I did extremely well in the summers, but business is slow in the winter, so I enrolled in an adult education class at the community college to learn stained glass window making and leading. I soon made it a part-time job. About that time I also went back to writing poetry and short stories about the love I felt for the hills. I lived alone contentedly for several years and then suddenly Mike moved back to Custer. Our friendship rekindled and the old destructive behavior began again.

Two years later, another family crisis brought us all back to Minnesota and this time I bought a small house in Sandstone. I continued to do massage and also work with stained glass. I specialized in free-standing sun catchers and concrete and stained glass stepping stones. Sandstone High School offered a wide variety of adult classes and so, over the next few years, I enrolled in taxidermy, woodwork and archery classes. I took evening classes in oil painting and did a collection of irises in bloom, which I still have to this day, many years later.

While living in Sandstone I became interested in city government. I served two terms on the city's planning commission. I'm proud to say I helped pass several important projects in that city.

Sandstone proved to be too close to the Hinckley casino and Mike began gambling. This was something I would not allow, so I asked him to leave. I could not afford to keep the house on my own and so I put it on the market. The house sold so quickly I didn't have time to find an apartment, so I ended up staying with a friend in Cottage Grove for the next six months. A unit became available in a senior apartment building in North Branch and I moved there in the autumn of 2004.

Within nine months, Mike had rented an apartment in the same building. He was now a serious diabetic with emphysema, but he continued to smoke and I slipped back into the old caretaking rut. This routine was taking a toll on my health as well. An apartment became available at a senior complex in Wyoming, Minnesota, one which I'd been waiting to get into since I'd left Cottage Grove, so I moved there in 2006. But again, Mike followed me, and as luck would have it, he moved into the apartment right across the hall from me. I was back to square one. His health was now continually deteriorating. He had already lost two toes due to diabetic complications.

That year I also had a medical set back. I was now 80 and after a routine health check-up, was told I had two aneurysms, one on the artery going into the heart and the other on an artery coming out. At first, I was devastated and the shock of it sent me into depression. I was prescribed an anti-depressant and experienced an extremely serious reaction. After I'd taken only two of the prescribed pills, I began to hallucinate and became suicidal.

Thank God I still had the presence of mind to call 911 and I was quickly taken to the psychiatric ward in a Minneapolis hospital where I spent two weeks in treatment and recovery. After I regained my perspective, I realized an aneurysm is not really that bad. After all, at my age, if one should rupture there will be no lingering. You're gone in ten minutes. What better way to exit?

Mike continued to get progressively worse. He had to have his right leg amputated just below the knee. He now needed more care than he could possibly receive at his apartment, even with the aid of a twice-a-week visiting county nurse. He had been in and out of hospitals so many times that year, he was finally moved to a convalescent facility in November 2010. Of course he didn't want to spend the rest of his life in a nursing home, he was only 70 years old. I certainly can't fault him for that, but he had nowhere else to go. I could do nothing more to help him.

It was at this time I learned he had been living a double life. During all of these years together, there had been another woman in the background. Fate stepped in and his friend from the shadows came forward. He left the care facility without being formally discharged and moved into her home to live with her. This turned out to be a godsend to him. He did not have to continue to stay in the nursing home, and he again had someone who actually loved him, taking care of him.

I have heard almost nothing from him since he moved into her home, but my true feelings are, "God bless her and I wish her luck."

Why Did I Continue?

Why did I continue to slip back into such destructive situations over and over?

Who knows? Maybe it was habit, or fear of change. Maybe it was really love. Or could it have been karma? We humans have no clue to the reason for all these unexplainable happenings in our lives.

Now that I am alone again, I sometimes wonder where I'd be if I hadn't become a widow, or if those damn horses hadn't run away. One fact is for sure--I would not have had all these memories to mull over or write about. And I will readily admit I have had amazing adventures, many close calls and memorable experiences.

My life has never been dull, but these episodes did not come knocking at my doors, I had to go out and make them happen. Yes, I've made many mistakes, and sometime I got a little closer to the edge than was wise, but I can honestly say I don't regret any of my side trips. Each incident, good or not so good, kept pointing me in this direction and played an important part in my journey to here.

Some of my favorite memories:

- I've owned and driven tandem dump trucks

- I've trained and bred horses

- I've ridden in the State Fair Parade and on search and rescue missions.

- I've traveled in a covered wagon train through the Black Hills.

- I've seen the western half of the United States from a fifth wheel camper.

- I've stood on the platform of an oil drilling rig and watched them cap a real well.

- I've worked the mounted patrol guarding a 1978 Hollywood movie set in rural Rush City, "A Christmas to Remember" starring Jason Robards and Eva Marie Saint. (It was a dud.)

- I worked one week as a fill-in tour guide on the historic 1880 train in Custer State Park. It travels the original route through the valleys and gorges from Hill City to Keystone.

- I've stood on a rail fence and watched the park rangers   round up hundreds of wild buffalo at the annual Autumn Buffalo Round-up.

And I was equally thrilled at every event.

Finally

When Mike moved from the nursing home to his friend's home, our story didn't end at that time, as I thought it would. During the five weeks he lived at her home, he did not contact either his son Mark or me. He didn't answer our phone calls or our messages, so we both assumed he had decided to cut all ties with us.

On the afternoon of April 12, 2012, he did finally call me. His voice sounded strong and friendly. It was around 4:00 p.m. and we talked about current news and unimportant things for around ten minutes.

Then he paused for a moment, and out of the clear blue sky he said, "We did have some really good times together, didn't we?"

I was surprised and I answered, "Yes we did. We have many, many good memories."

He cleared his throat as if he might be a little choked up, and then he was quiet again, as if thinking. We spoke a minute or two more and then said our good-byes and hung up. The last thing I said to him was, "be sure to call Mark, he's feeling a bit abandoned," and he said he would.

After hanging up, I quickly called his son to tell him his dad would be calling him soon. About an hour and a half later I got a call back and the caller ID said it was Mark. I assumed he was calling to tell me his dad had called, but when I answered, he was crying and through his tears he stammered, "Dad is dead. He's dead. They just called me and said he's dead. He died twenty minutes ago."

I was stunned. I couldn't believe it. I had just spoken to him. He had sounded fine. I learned later that evening that I was the only person he had called.

In a way, I was comforted. We'd had a friendly and peaceful closure. I felt perhaps all those years we'd spent together and all the experiences we'd shared and the fun we had was actually important to him after all.

Coat Of Many Colors

I have moved throughout the United States and have seen quite a bit of the country. Now here I am, back in Minnesota. I've completed life's full circle, and at 83, if I must settle, I guess this is as friendly an area as I will find.

I am grateful my apartment is warm in the winter and cool in the summer (as long as the A/C keeps working). My family, which is quite large now, with three sons, nine grandchildren and eleven great-grandkids, all live within a day's traveling distance. I'm still fairly healthy. I've got my own teeth and my hearing is exceptionally good. And though my hair is pure white, it's still thick. My mind seems pretty clear, most of the time anyway. So what more could an old woman ask for?

Every enterprise I've entered into, every quest I have undertaken and all the problems I've been forced to face have made me who I am today. I've come to believe that every experience spins another thread to be woven into the fabric that tells the stories of a life. My cloth is unique unlike any other, it is a splash of brilliant colors and a multitude of designs. Some threads are twisted and worn. Some are frayed. Some are broken and repaired with knots. The design isn't perfect, but neither is life.

In my final presentation, I will proudly display my coat of many colors. I will wrap it tightly around my shoulders and announce: "This is my robe. It tells my story. This is who I am."

-Laurel Carey

ABOUT THE AUTHOR

Laurel Carey was born in a small Minnesota town during the Great Depression in 1929. Her family moved to Minneapolis at the beginning of World War 2 where she met and married her high school sweetheart in 1948. The couple had three healthy sons.

In the 1970's they bought a 120-acre hobby farm where they raised a menagerie of animals and lived happily for almost ten years. Their sons all married and started their own lives.

In August 1983, Laurel found herself a widow at 54 years old when her husband Bernie lost his year long battle with cancer. It was at this time in her life she became interested in writing. She started with poetry, then moved to children's stories in rhyme and on to short stories.

The gypsy feet of her youth started itching and she eventually sold the farm to one of her sons and began her life long desire to explore new horizons. The second half of her life has found her constantly on the move, living in 12 different locations west of the Mississippi River. Traveling and exploring are her passions and writing about these adventures is her reward.

Now in her twilight years, she is living in a senior apartment complex in Wyoming, Minnesota. But for how long? Who knows? Lately she has been experiencing an advanced case of Restless Feet Syndrome and may start seeking out new adventures in the years ahead.

24568720R00068

Made in the USA
Charleston, SC
26 November 2013